ART OF JAPANESE WRITING & CALLIGRAPHY
KANJI. HIRAGANA. KATAKANA

ART OF JAPANESE WRITING & CALLIGRAPHY
KANJI. HIRAGANA. KATAKANA

BY: HIDEO MURANAKA

ISBN# 1-58721-148-3

1stBooks - rev. 03/22/00

About the Book

    This textbook is a summary of an introductory study of Japanese calligraphy for college students. It includes brush writing systems of Kanji (Chinese characters) and a Japanese syllabary (Hiragana or Katakana).

    This book will help students comprehend Japanese calligraphic historical information makes it easier and more interesting for students to practice writing characters with brush and ink.

Preface

For some time I have thought it would be helpful to write an introductory study of Japanese calligraphy for my college students. This book has grown out of that idea.

Japanese calligraphy dates back to the 3rd or 4th century A.D. In Japan we use Chinese characters as well as the Japanese syllabary of Hiragana and Katakana. After the official introduction of Kanji(Chinese characters) to Japan in the 6th century A.D., Chinese calligraphy systems spread all over Japan.

The Japanese people responded to a growing need to develop their own syllabary in order to read Chinese phrases which have different sentence structure. The most popular calligraphic style is the O GI SHI(Wang Hsi Chih) tradition.

I will introduce a variety of Chinese and Japanese calligraphic styles to help students' understanding of brush-writing systems. Choose your favorite calligraphic manner and develop your own brush and ink writing style.

Enjoy this ancient art form as creative and thoughtful expression.

Hideo Muranaka

California State University
1999

Table of Contents

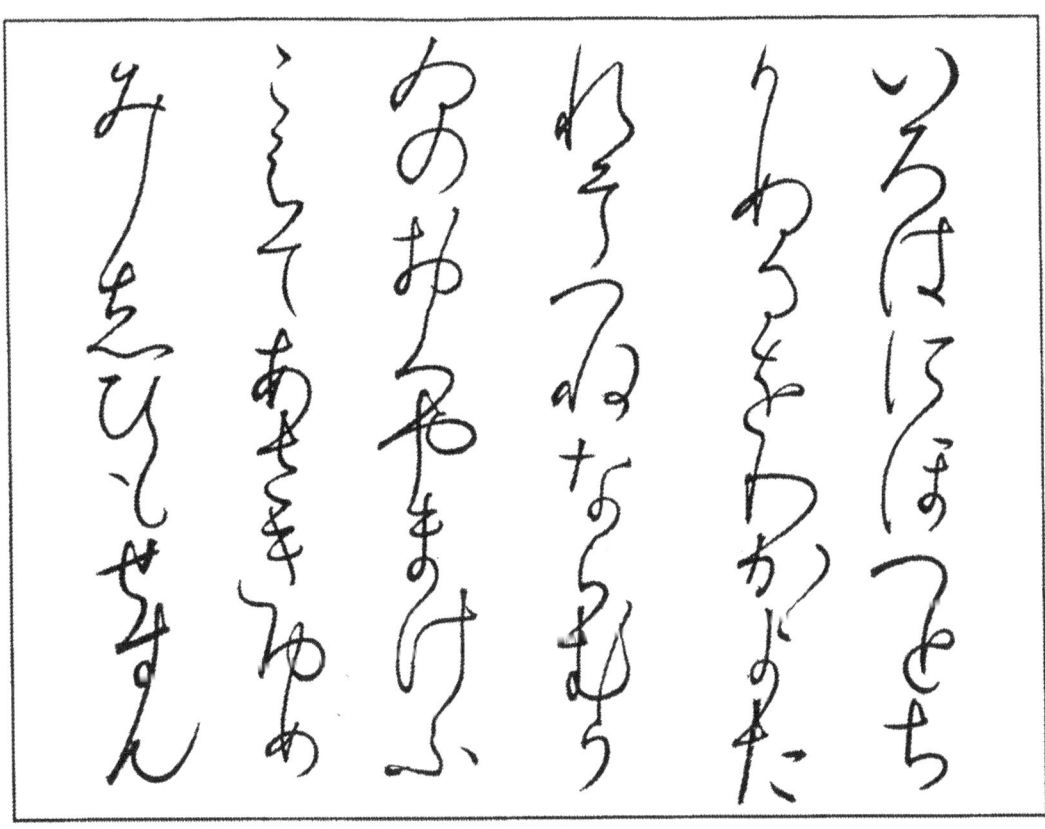

【The Poem】	【Romanization】	【Kana Represented】
いろはにほへど	Iro wa nioedo	I-ro ha ni-ho-he-to
ちりぬるを	Chirinuru o	Chi-ri-nu-ru (w)o
わがよたれぞ	Waga yo tare zo	Wa-ka yo ta-re so
つねならむ	Tsune naran	Tsu-ne na-ra-mu
うゐのおくやま	Ui no okuyama	U-(w)i no o-ku-ya-ma
けふこえて	Kyo koete	Ke-fu Ko-e-te
あさきゆめみじ	Asaki yume miji	A-sa-ki yu-me mi-shi
ゑひもせず（ん）	Ei mo sezu	(W)e-hi mo se-su (N)

THE I-RO-HA UTA   "Flowers are fragrant, but they fade away. So much happen in our world, yet nothing lasts forever. Climbing the high mountains always brings you back to the valleys. You will have no more shallow dreams or temptations. You always come back to nomal.

Classification of Kana (Hiragana, Katakana) - (1)
The Transformation from Chinese Characters to Japanese Syllabary

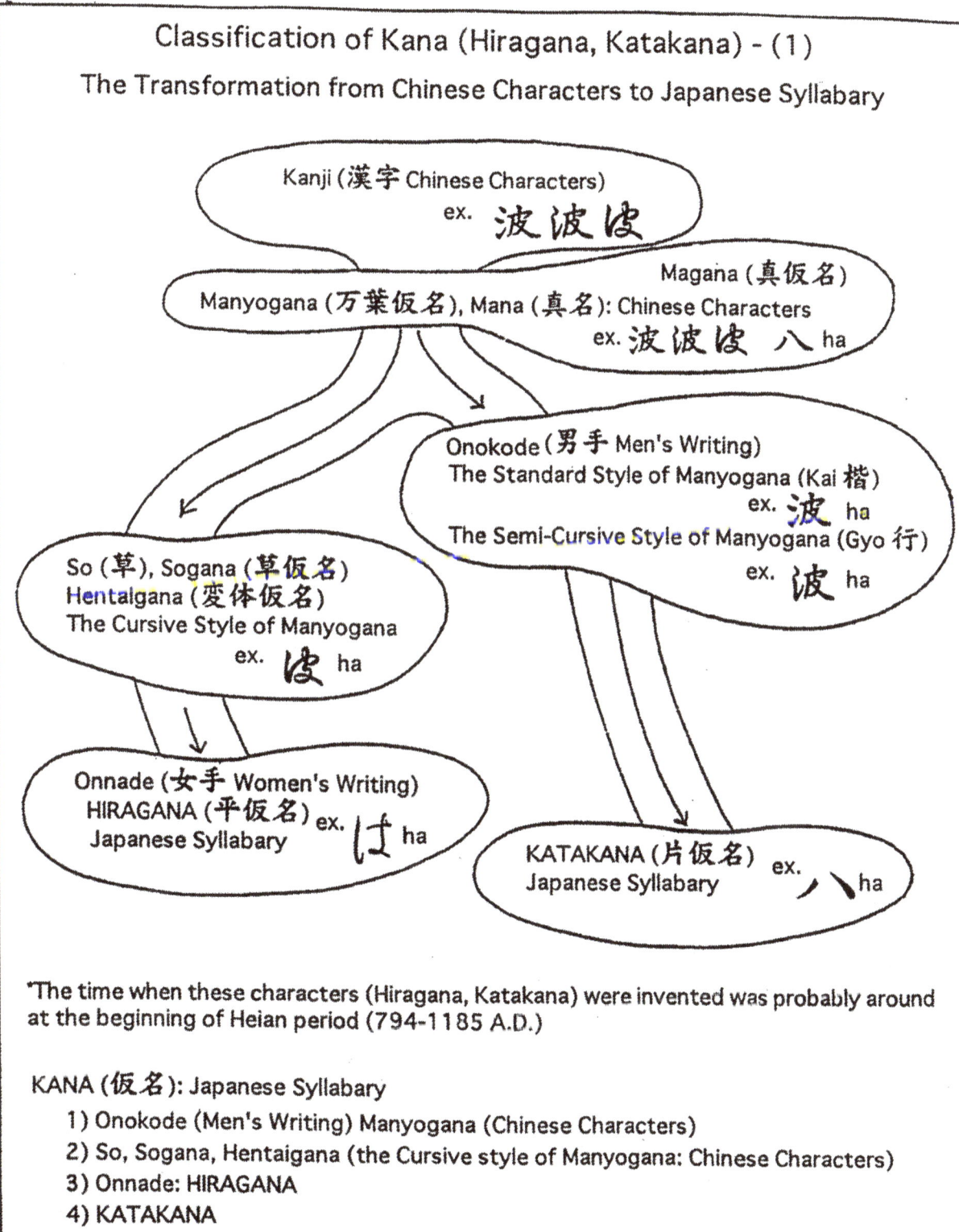

*The time when these characters (Hiragana, Katakana) were invented was probably around at the beginning of Heian period (794-1185 A.D.)

KANA (仮名): Japanese Syllabary

1) Onokode (Men's Writing) Manyogana (Chinese Characters)
2) So, Sogana, Hentaigana (the Cursive style of Manyogana: Chinese Characters)
3) Onnade: HIRAGANA
4) KATAKANA

Classification of Kana (Hiragana, Katakana) - (2)

Since the introduction of Kanji (Chinese Characters), Japanese used Chinese Characters and Chinese Phrases for daily writing, but it was very difficult for the common Japanese people. During Heian period (794-1185 A.D.), Japanese men mainly used Chinese Characters to write a letter and a record as their refinement. The Japanese women often wrote their poems and love letters in Hiragana. Court ladies applied these characters for the upper class correspondence in their daily writing.

*Manyogana: means Kanji (Chinese Characters) were used as a phonetic sign to read Chinese Phrases. This means to ignore the meaning of Kanji and take only a sound of a Chinese Character as an alphabet.

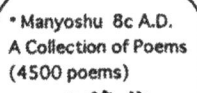
* Manyoshu 8c A.D.
A Collection of Poems
(4500 poems)
万葉集

ex.  ha

1) Onokode: Men's Writing
The Standard Style of Manyogana (Kai 楷)
The Semi-Cursive Style of Manyogana (Gyo 行)

ex.  ha

2) So
   Sogana
   Hentaigana

indicates Cursive manner of
Manyogana (Chinese Characters)

ex.  ha

3) Onnade: means Women's Writing (HIRAGANA). HIRAGANA was
a simplified form of Cursive manner of Manyogana.

ex.  ha

4) KATAKANA: means half of a Kanji or part of a Kanji character.
Since Nara period (710-794 A.D.) Kanji was used as a phonetic sign
or returning mark to read Chinese phrases.
KATAKANA is a simplified form of Standard style of Kanji.

ex.  ha

*Sanpitsu (三筆) and Sanseki (三蹟)

In the Heian (平安) period, 794-1192, there was a tremendous achievement in religion, study, literature and art. Especially, in the field of calligraphy, the outstanding calligraphers appeared in this period, so called Sanpitsu (三筆 Three Brush Strokes) and Sanseki (三蹟 Three Touches of Calligraphy). Sanseki are well-known in Wayo (和様) Style. Sanseki and Sanpitsu are listed below.

*Sanpitsu (三筆)

    1) Saga Tenno (嵯峨天皇) Emperor Saga, 786-842

    2) Kukai (空海) 774-835

    3) Tachibana no Hayanari (橘逸勢) ?-842

*Sanseki (三蹟)

    1) Onono Michikaze (To fu) (小野道風), 894-966

    2) Fujiwara, Sukemasa (藤原佐理), 944-998

    3) Fujiwara, Yukinari (藤原行成), 972-1027

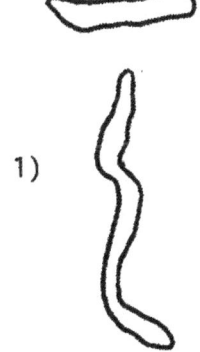
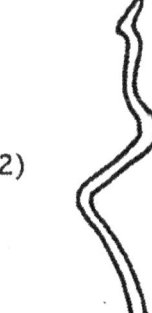
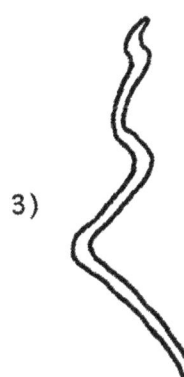

1)   2)   3)

JAPANESE CHRONOLOGICAL TABLE

Ca. 10,000 B.C. JOMON (縄文) Period

300: Beginning of YAYOI (弥生) Period

250: Beginning of KOFUN (古墳) Period

539-644 ASUKA (飛鳥) Period

645-710 HAKUHO (白鳳) Period

710-794 NARA (奈良) Period

794-1185 HEIAN (平安) Period or FUJIWARA (藤原)

1185-1392 KAMAKURA (鎌倉) Period

1392-1573 MUROMACHI (室町) Period or ASHIKAGA (足利)

1573-1603 MOMOYAMA (桃山) Period

1603-1868 EDO (江戸) Period or TOKUGAWA (徳川)

1868-1912 MEIJI (明治) Period

1912-1926 TAISHO (大正) Period

1926-1989 SHOWA (昭和) Period

1989- HEISEI (平成) Period

B.C.
300
200
100
0
100
200
300
400
500
600
700
800
900
1000
1100
1200
1300
1400
1500
1600
1700
1800
1900
A.D.

	Katakana	Stroke Order		Katakana	Stroke Order
i	イ		wa	ワ	
ro	ロ		ka	カ	
ha	ハ		yo	ヨ	
ni	ニ		ta	タ	
ho	ホ		re	レ	
he	ヘ		so	ソ	
to	ト		tsu	ツ	
chi	チ		ne	ネ	
ri	リ		na	ナ	
nu	ヌ		ra	ラ	
ru	ル		mu	ム	
o	ヲ		u	ウ	

	Katakana	Stroke Order		Katakana	Stroke Order
i	ヰ		sa	サ	
no	ノ		ki	キ	
o	オ		yu	ユ	
ku	ク		me	メ	
ya	ヤ		mi	ミ	
ma	マ		shi	シ	
ke	ケ		e	エ	
fu	フ		hi	ヒ	
ko	コ		mo	モ	
e	エ		se	セ	
te	テ		su	ス	
a	ア		n	ン	

The Transformation of " Hiragana "

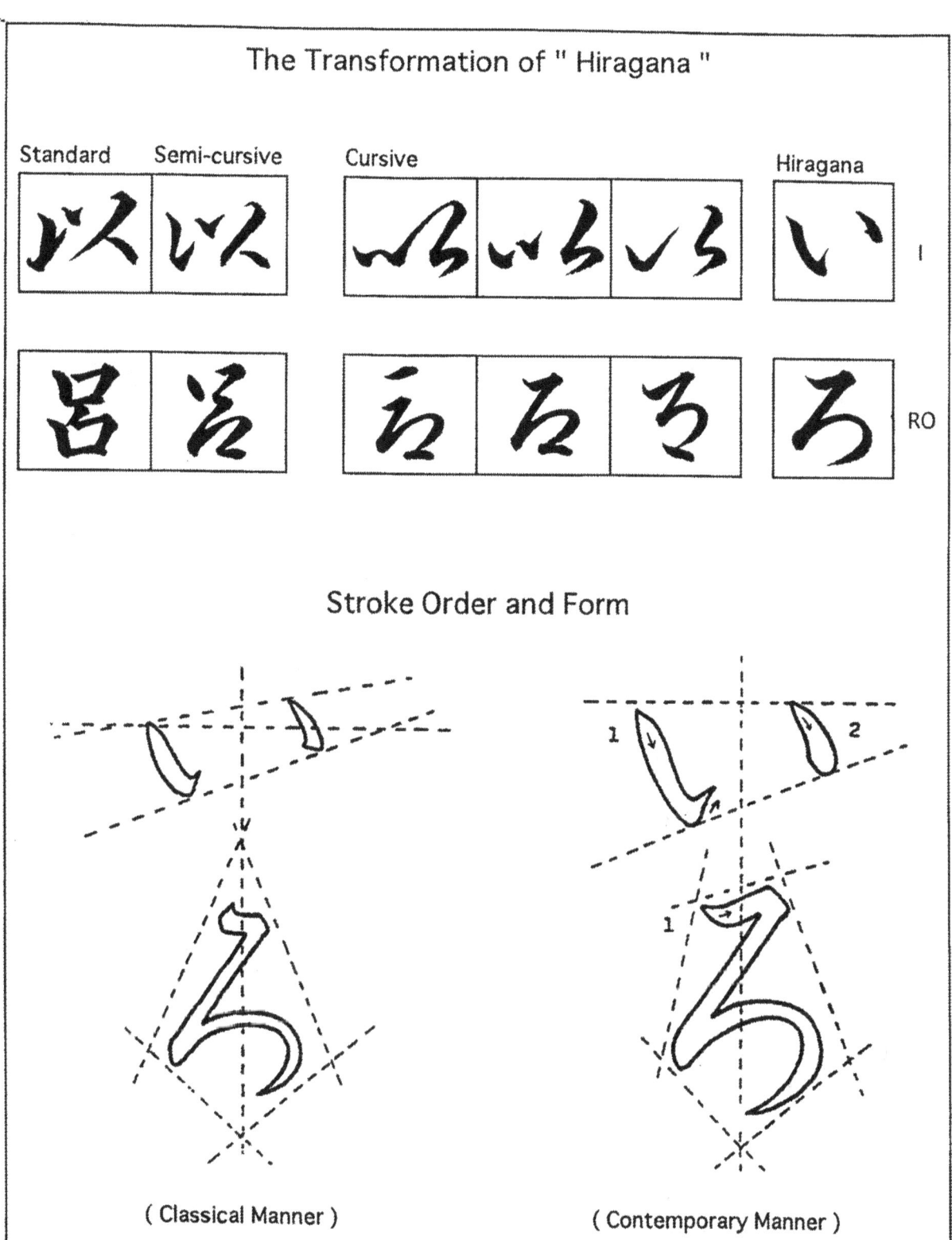

Standard   Semi-cursive   Cursive   Hiragana

I

RO

Stroke Order and Form

(Classical Manner)   (Contemporary Manner)

The Transformation of " Hiragana "

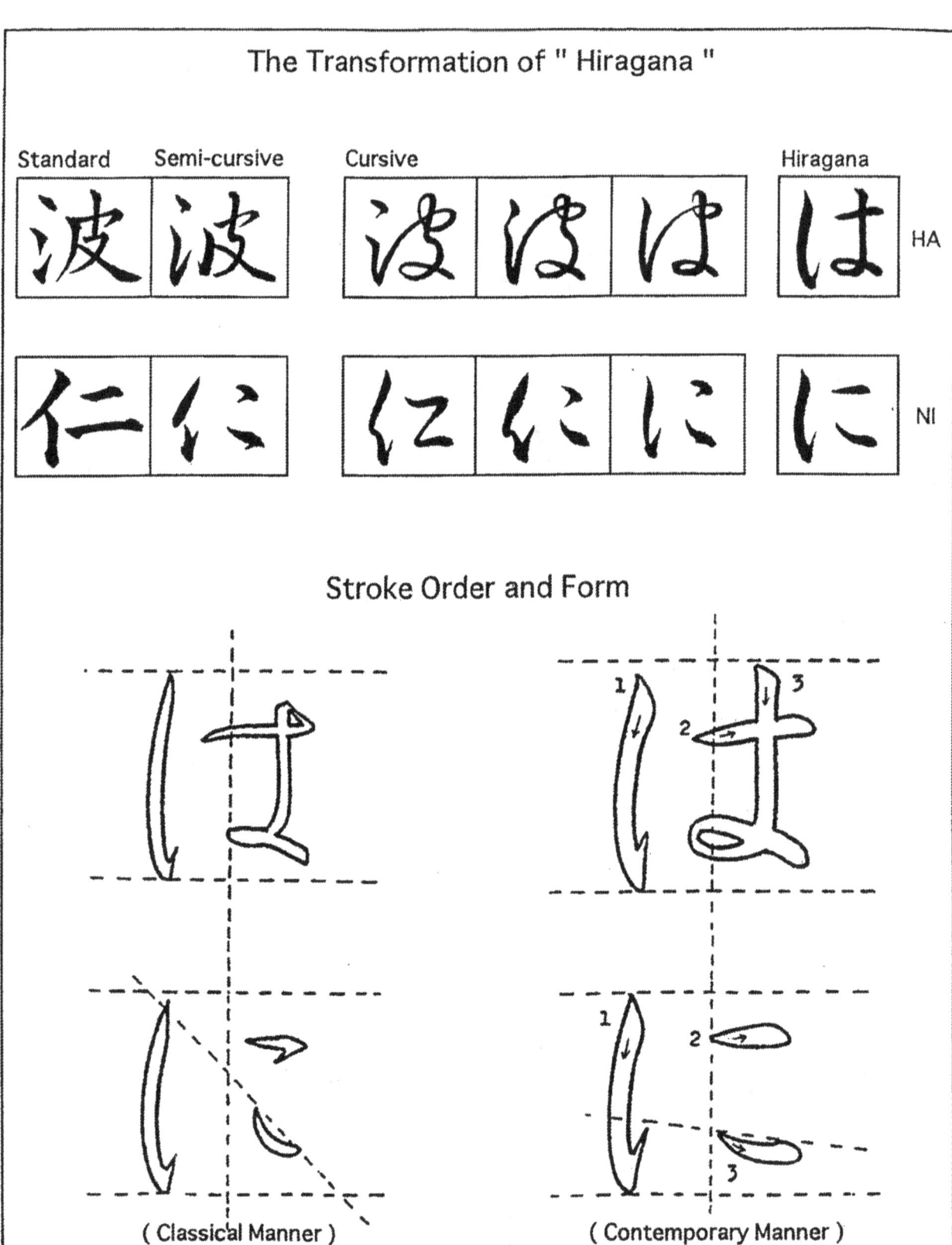

Standard	Semi-cursive	Cursive			Hiragana	
波	波	波	は	は	は	HA
仁	仁	仁	に	に	に	NI

Stroke Order and Form

(Classical Manner)   (Contemporary Manner)

The Transformation of " Hiragana "

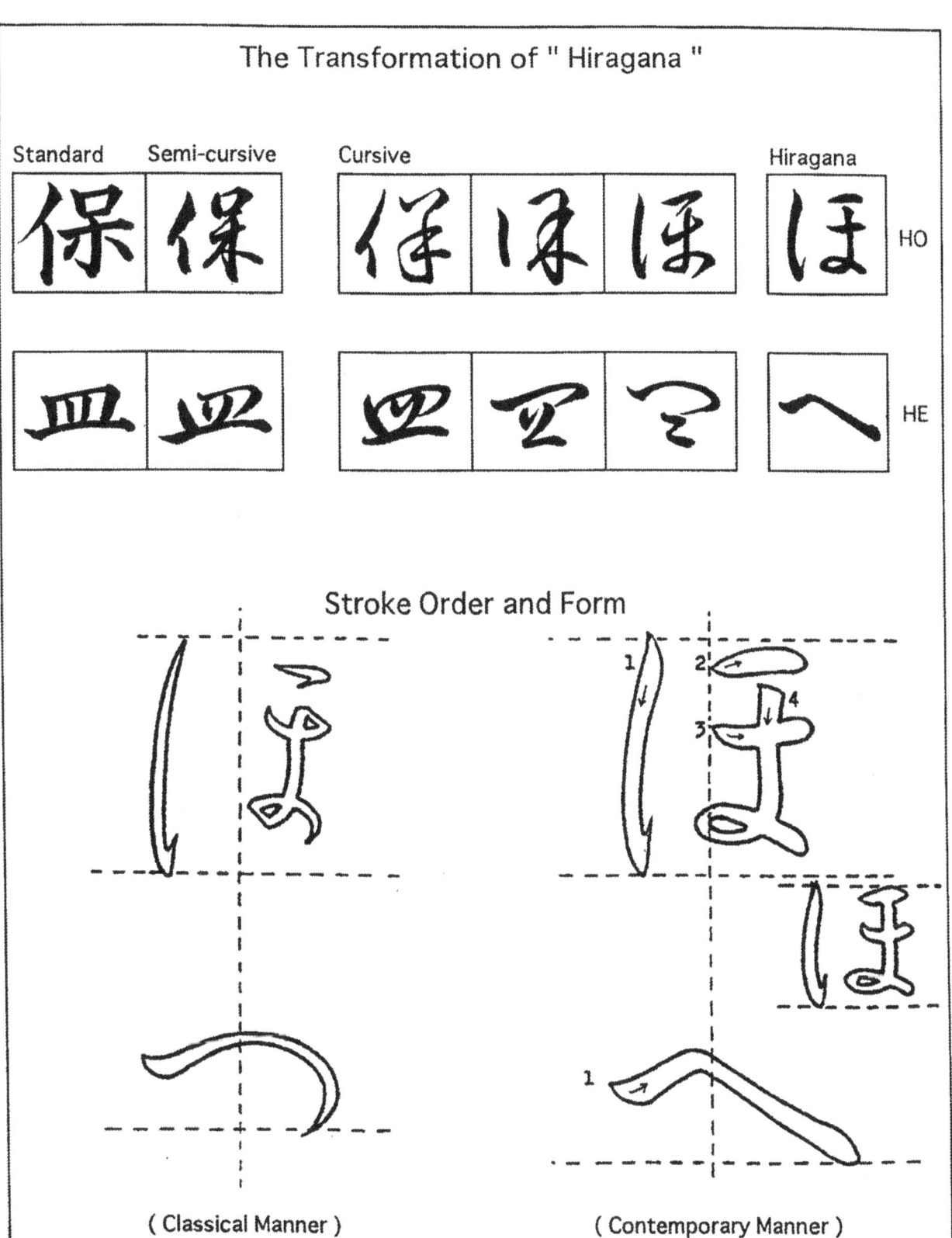

Standard Semi-cursive Cursive Hiragana

保 保 保 床 活 ほ HO

皿 皿 皿 亚 乙 へ HE

Stroke Order and Form

(Classical Manner) (Contemporary Manner)

The Transformation of " Hiragana "

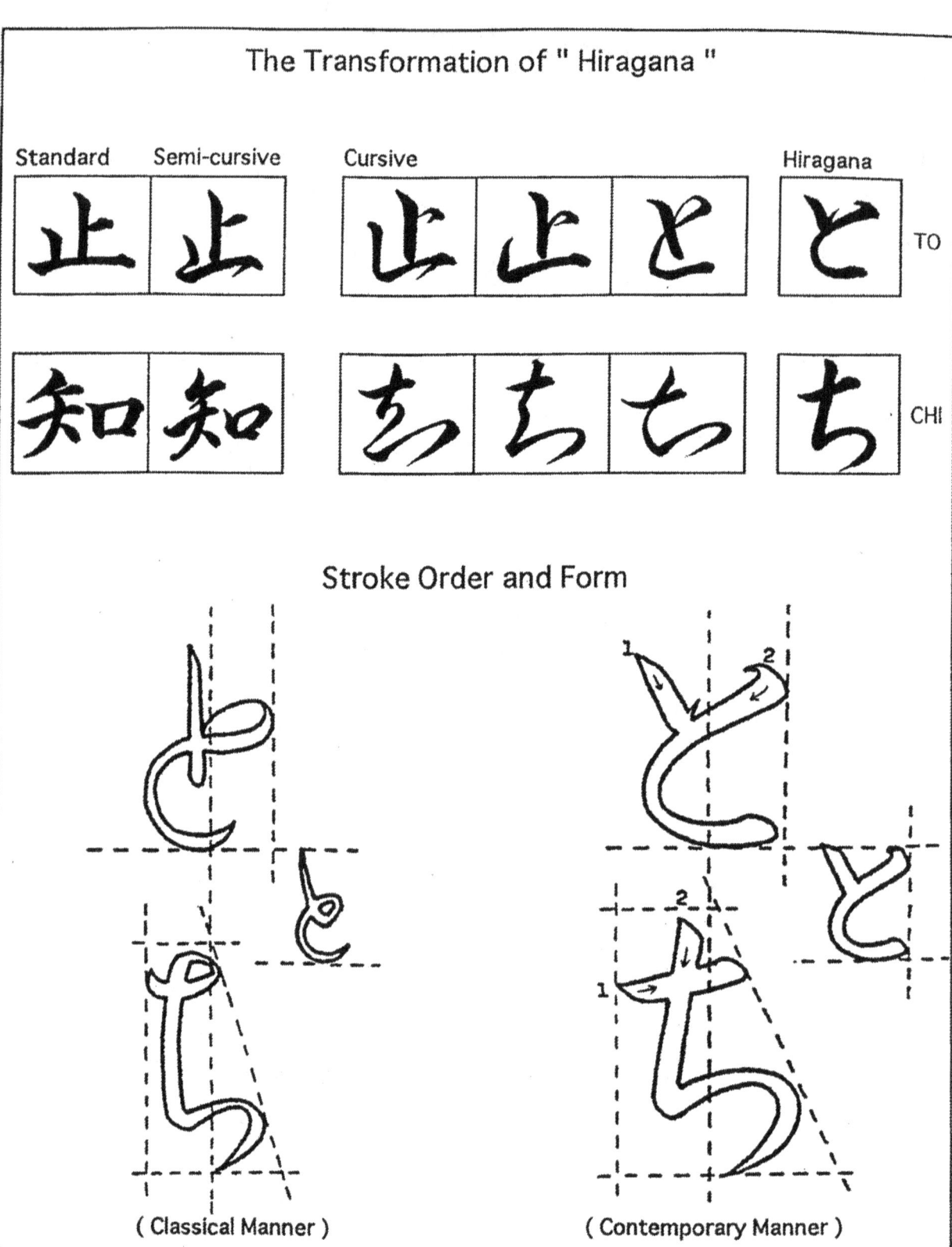

Standard	Semi-cursive	Cursive			Hiragana	
止	止	止	止	と	と	TO
知	知		ち	ち	ち	ち	CHI

Stroke Order and Form

(Classical Manner)   (Contemporary Manner)

The Transformation of " Hiragana "

Standard	Semi-cursive	Cursive			Hiragana	

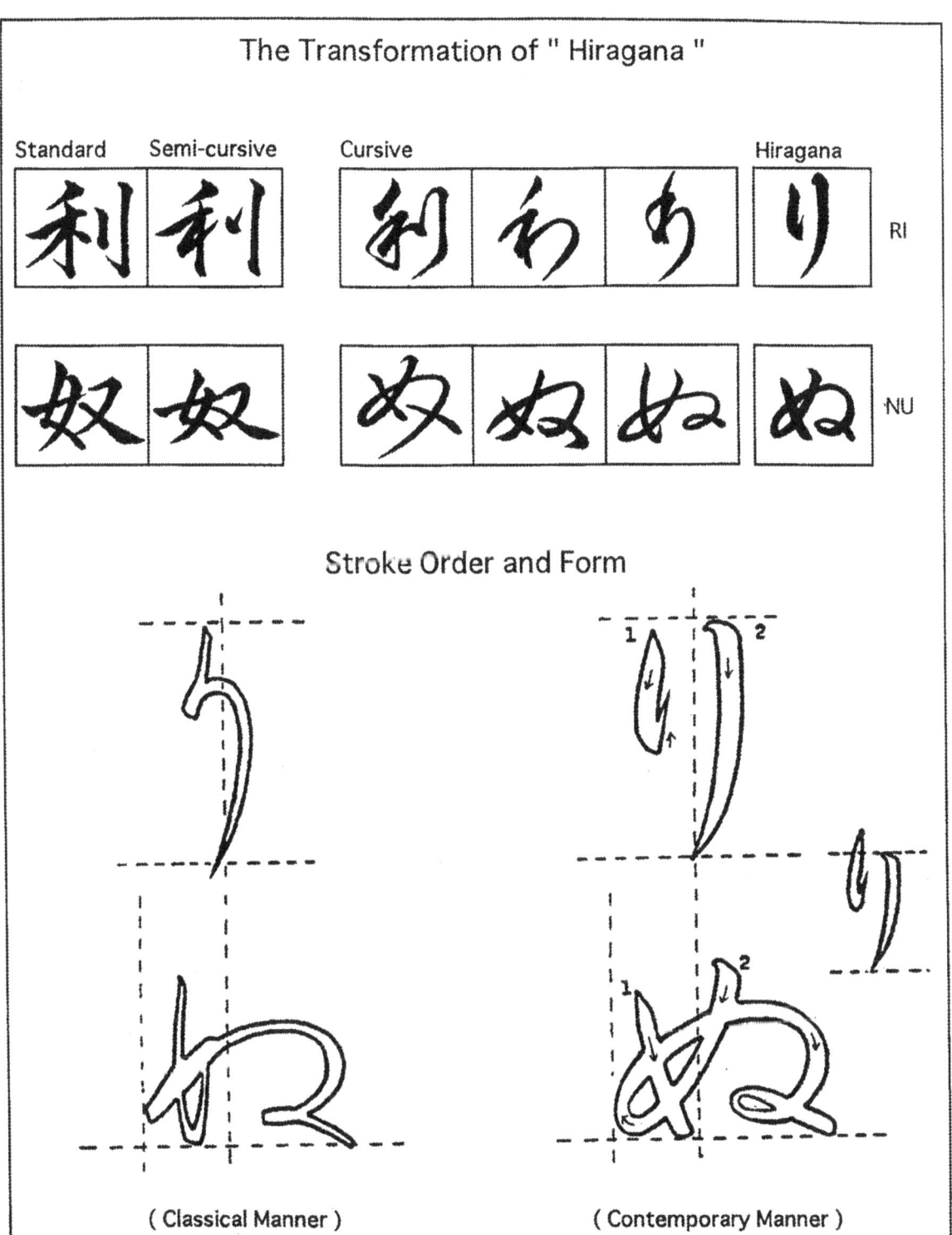

						RI
利	利	利	わ	あ	り	
						NU
奴	奴	奴	ぬ	ぬ	ぬ	

Stroke Order and Form

(Classical Manner) (Contemporary Manner)

19

The Transformation of " Hiragana "

Standard	Semi-cursive	Cursive			Hiragana	
留	留	㽞	㽞	る	る	RU
遠	遠	遠	㐬	を	を	O

Stroke Order and Form

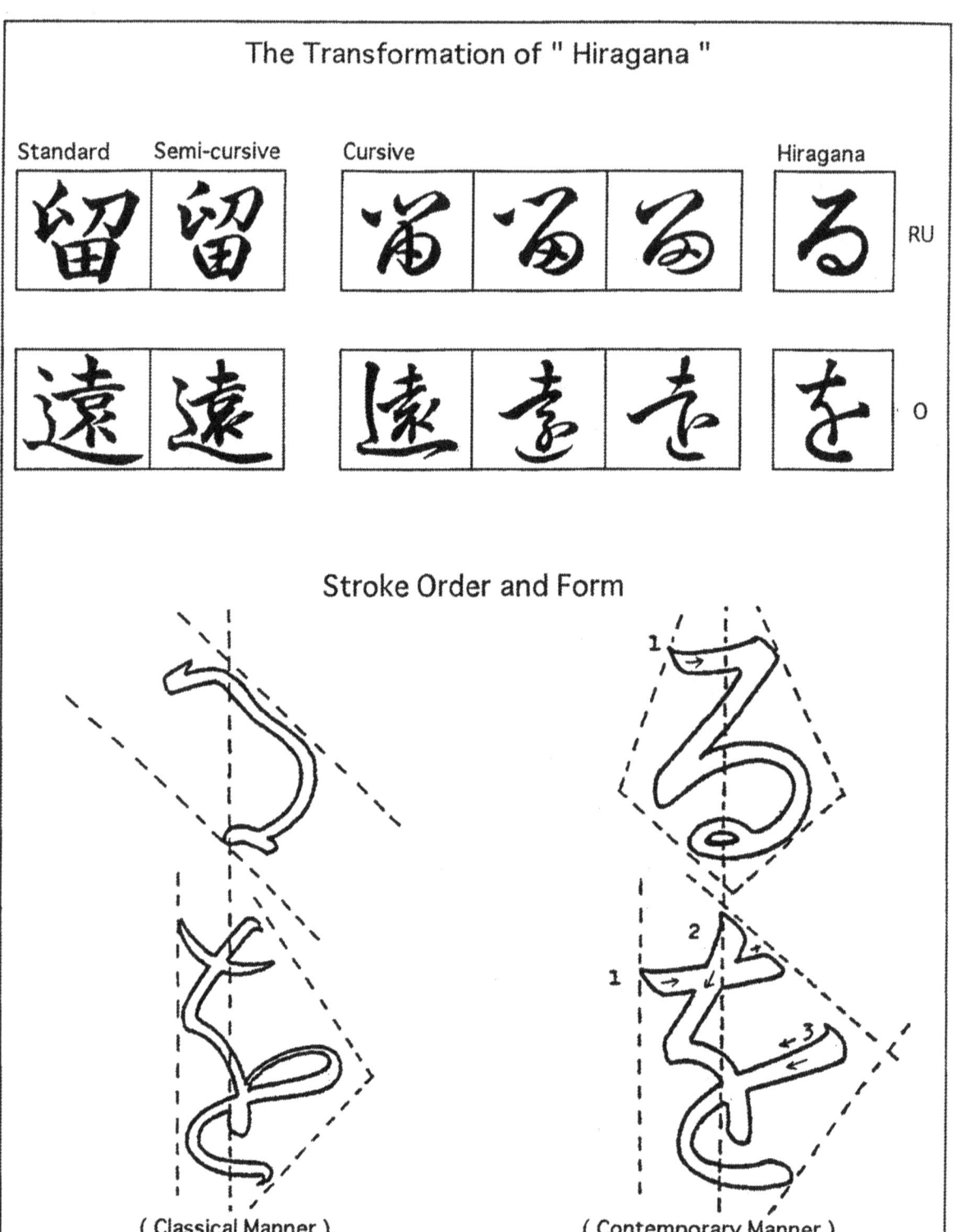

(Classical Manner)   (Contemporary Manner)

The Transformation of " Hiragana "

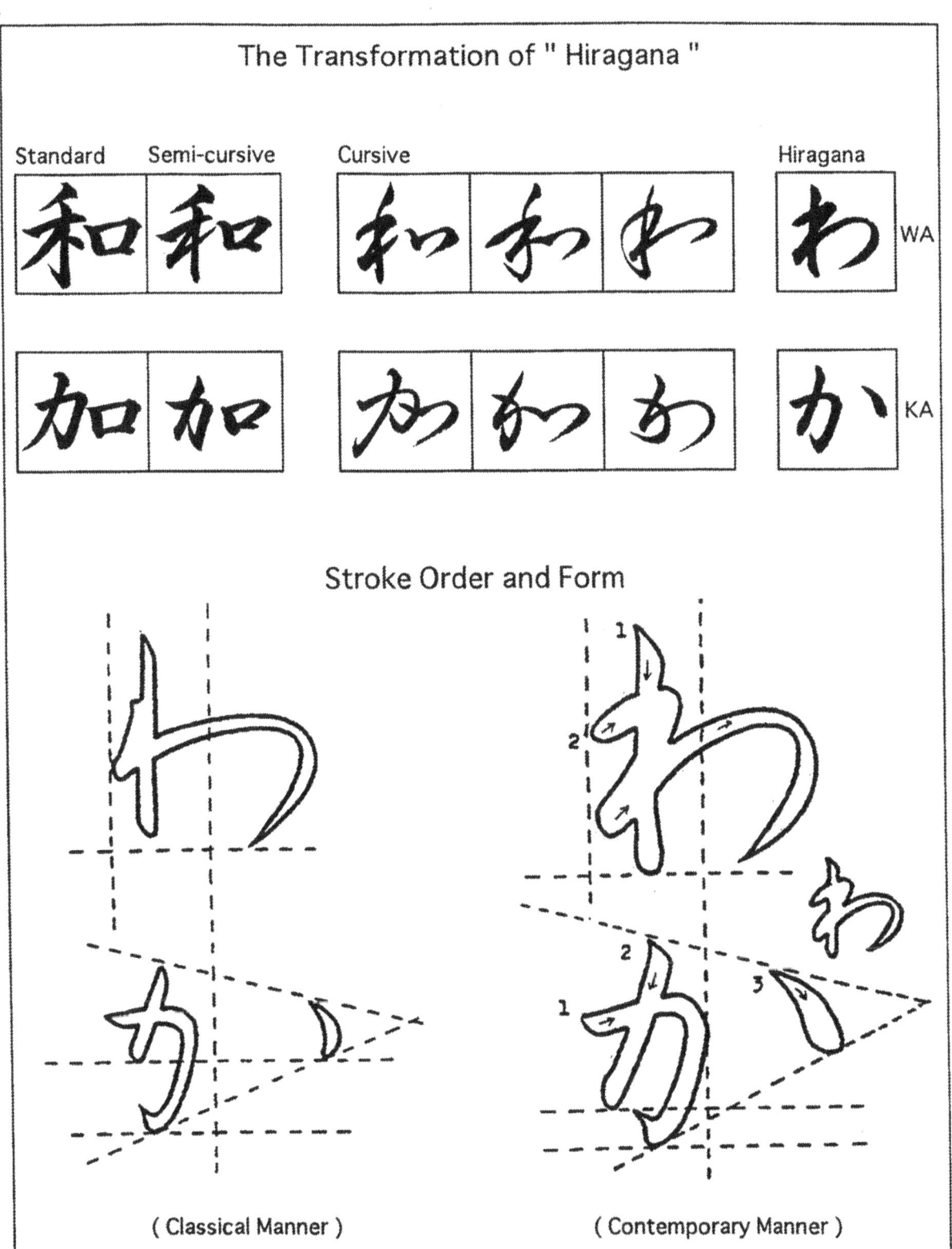

Standard Semi-cursive Cursive   Hiragana

和 和   和 和 わ   わ WA

加 加   か わ わ   か KA

Stroke Order and Form

(Classical Manner)   (Contemporary Manner)

21

The Transformation of " Hiragana "

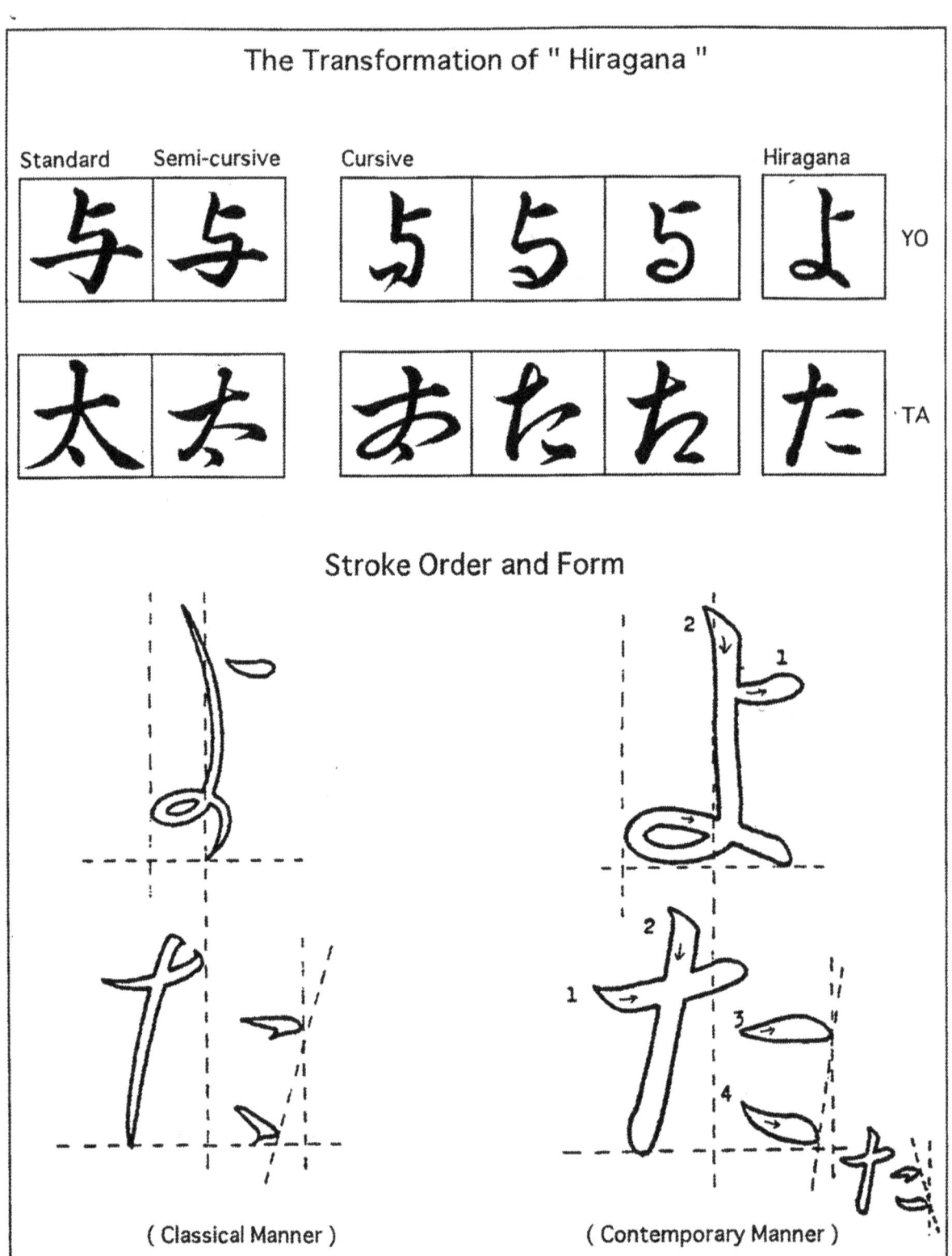

Standard	Semi-cursive	Cursive			Hiragana
与	与	与	与	与	よ	YO
太	太	あ	た	た	た	TA

Stroke Order and Form

(Classical Manner)　　　　　　　　(Contemporary Manner)

22

The Transformation of " Hiragana "

Standard	Semi-cursive	Cursive			Hiragana	

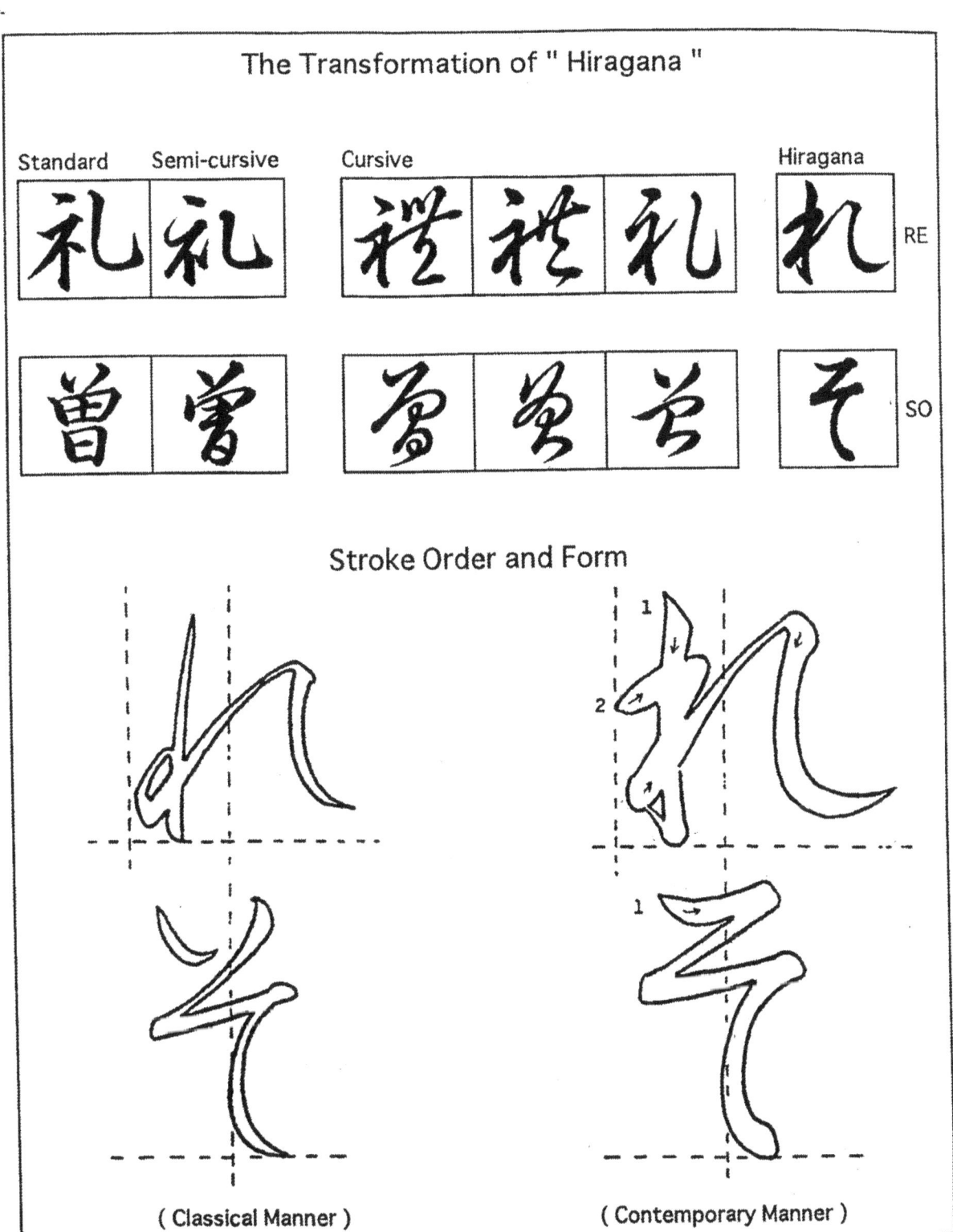

RE

SO

Stroke Order and Form

(Classical Manner)

(Contemporary Manner)

The Transformation of " Hiragana "

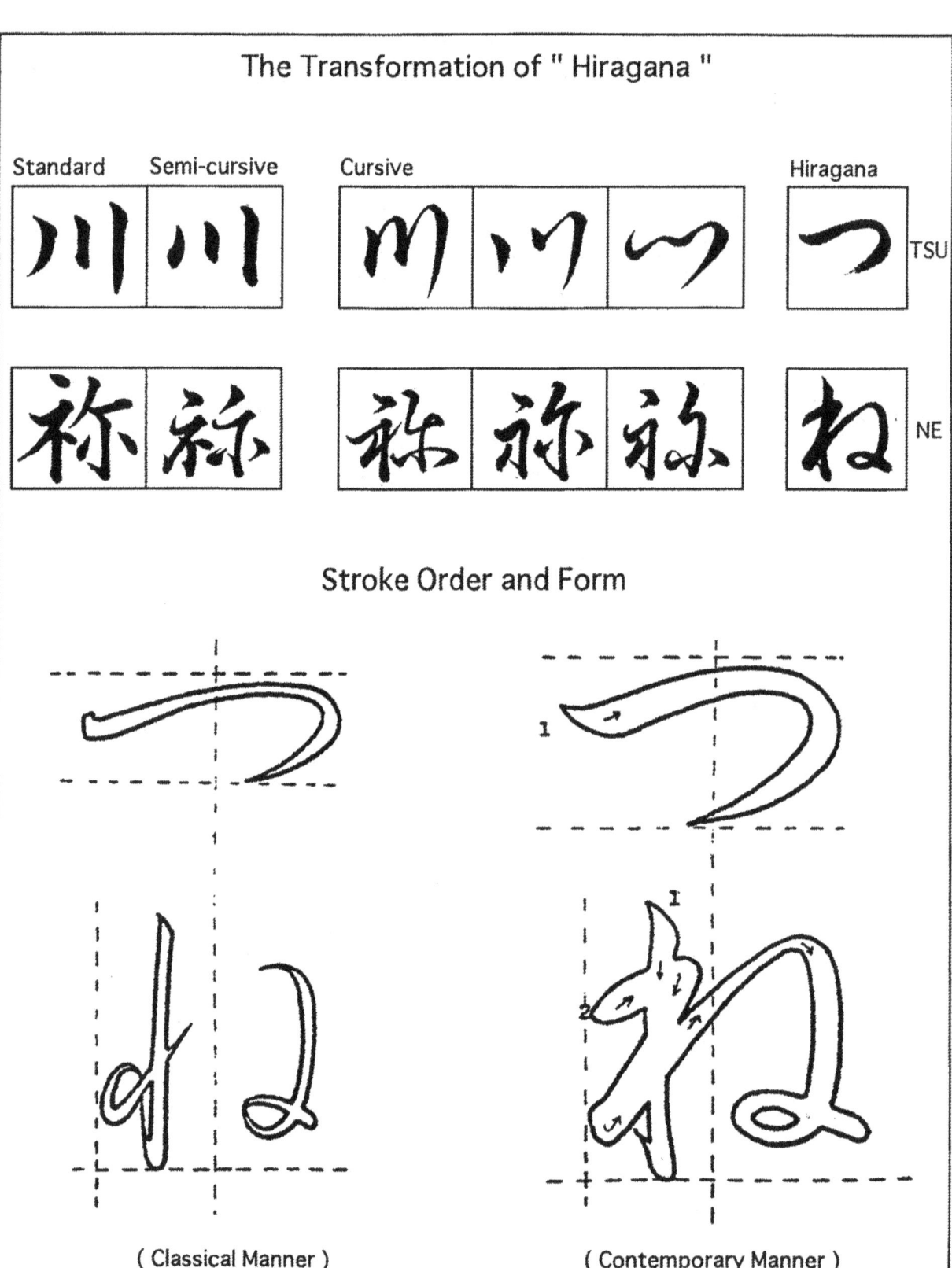

Standard	Semi-cursive	Cursive			Hiragana
川	川	川	ツ	つ	つ TSU
祢	祢	祢	祢	祢	ね NE

Stroke Order and Form

(Classical Manner)

(Contemporary Manner)

The Transformation of " Hiragana "

Standard	Semi-cursive	Cursive			Hiragana	

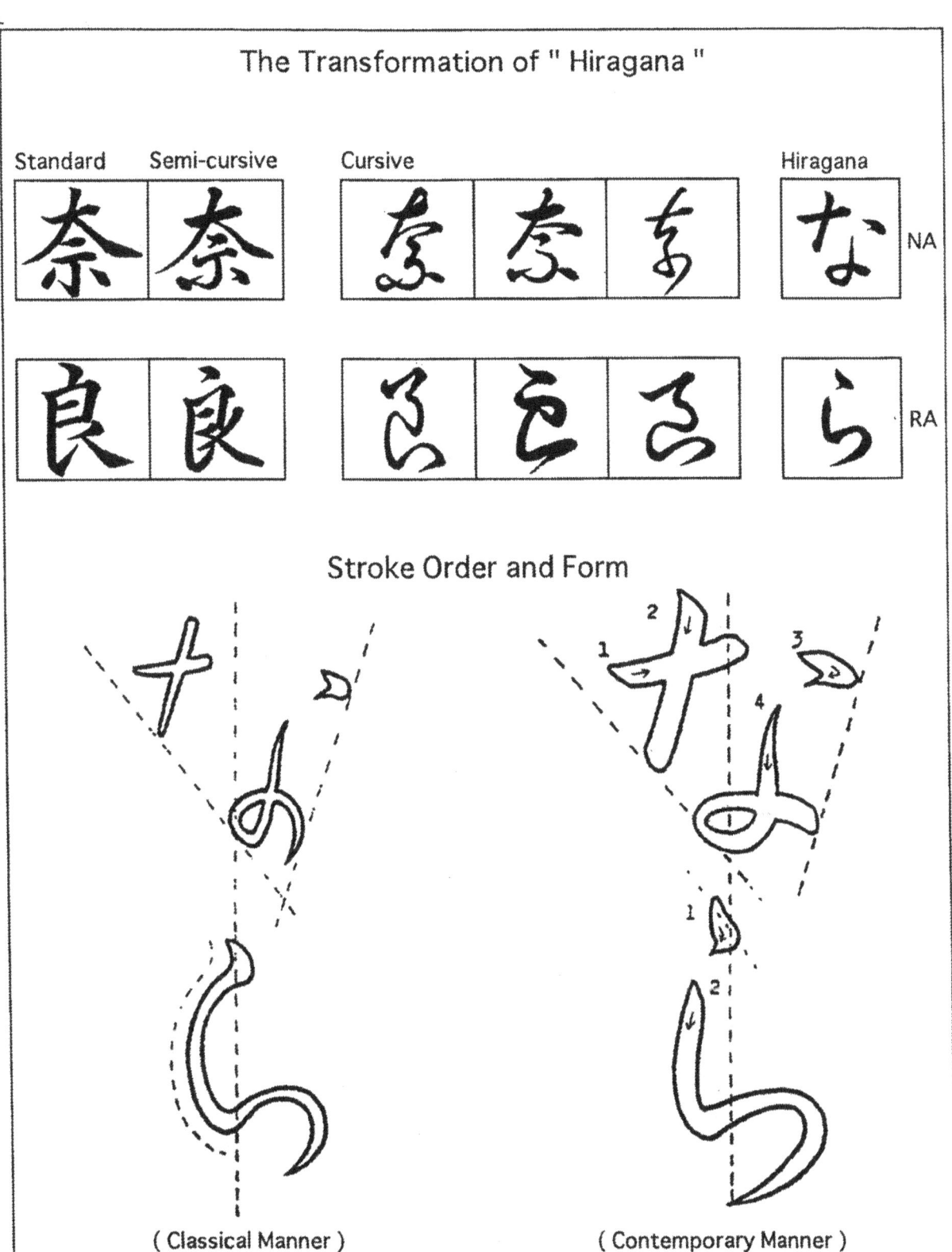

Standard   Semi-cursive   Cursive   Hiragana

奈　奈　　奈　奈　す　　な　NA

良　良　　ら　ミ　ら　　ら　RA

Stroke Order and Form

(Classical Manner)   (Contemporary Manner)

The Transformation of " Hiragana "

Standard Semi-cursive Cursive Hiragana

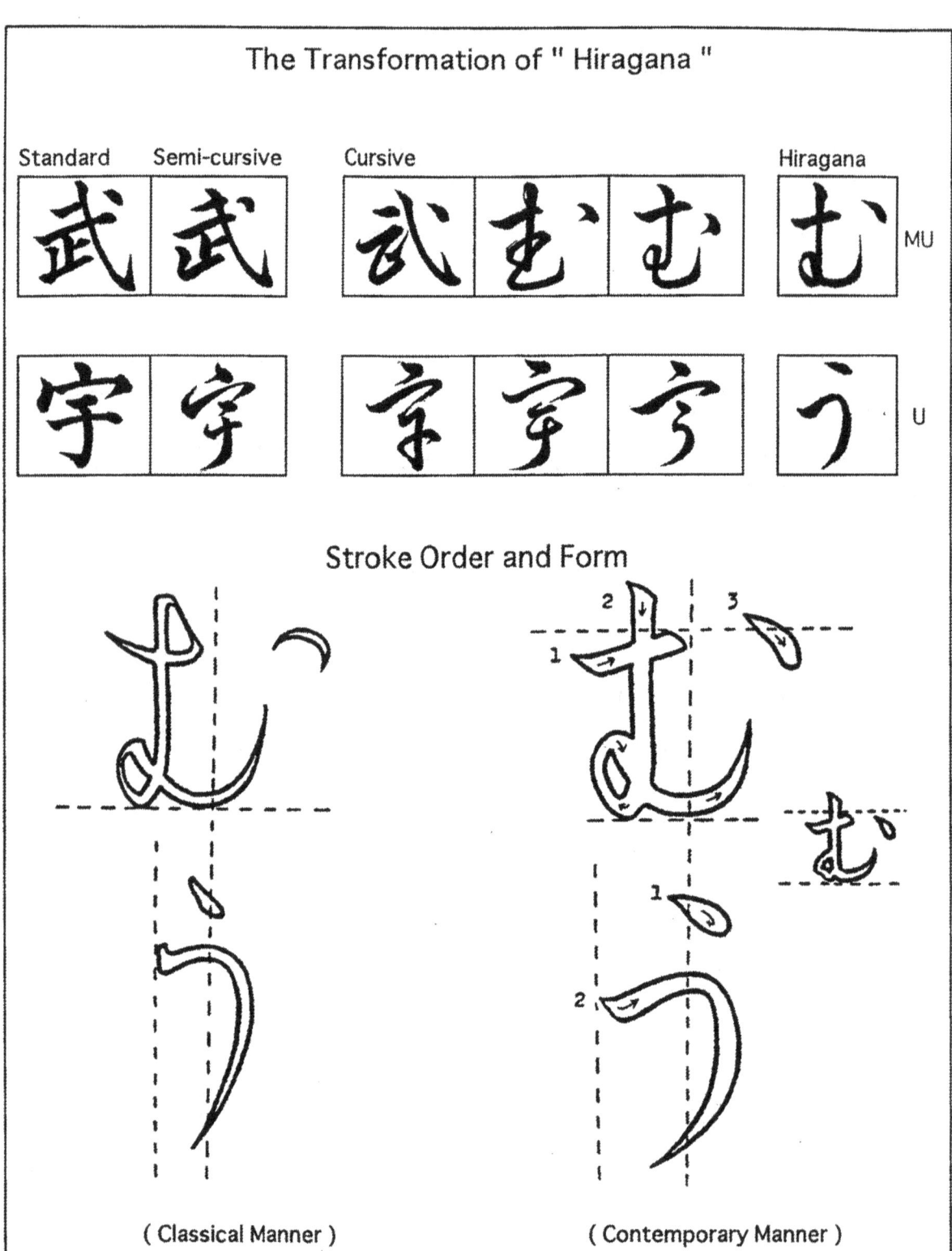

MU

U

Stroke Order and Form

(Classical Manner)　　　　(Contemporary Manner)

The Transformation of " Hiragana "

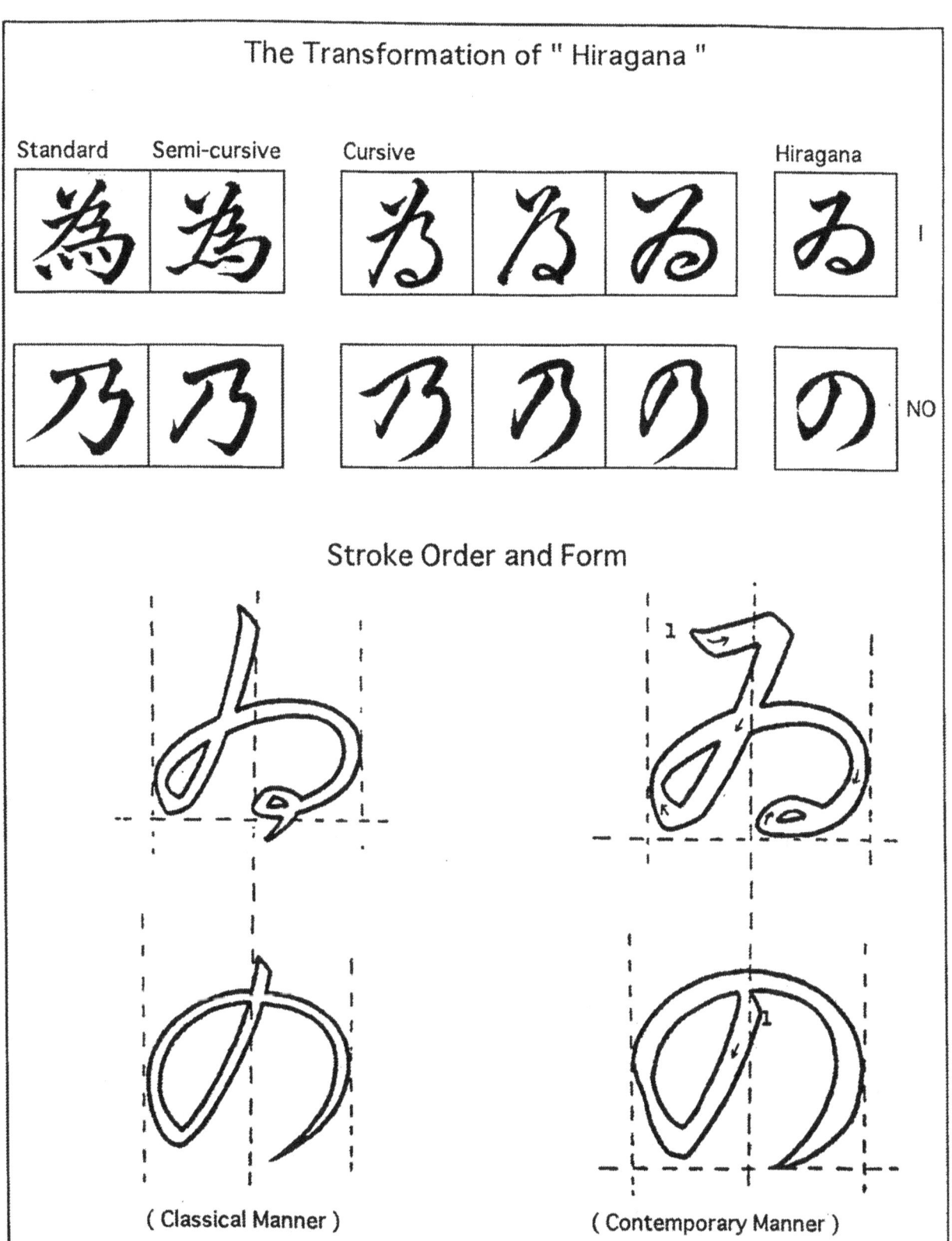

Standard Semi-cursive Cursive Hiragana

為 為 为 为 る る | I

乃 乃 乃 乃 の の NO

Stroke Order and Form

(Classical Manner) (Contemporary Manner)

The Transformation of " Hiragana "

Standard	Semi-cursive	Cursive			Hiragana	

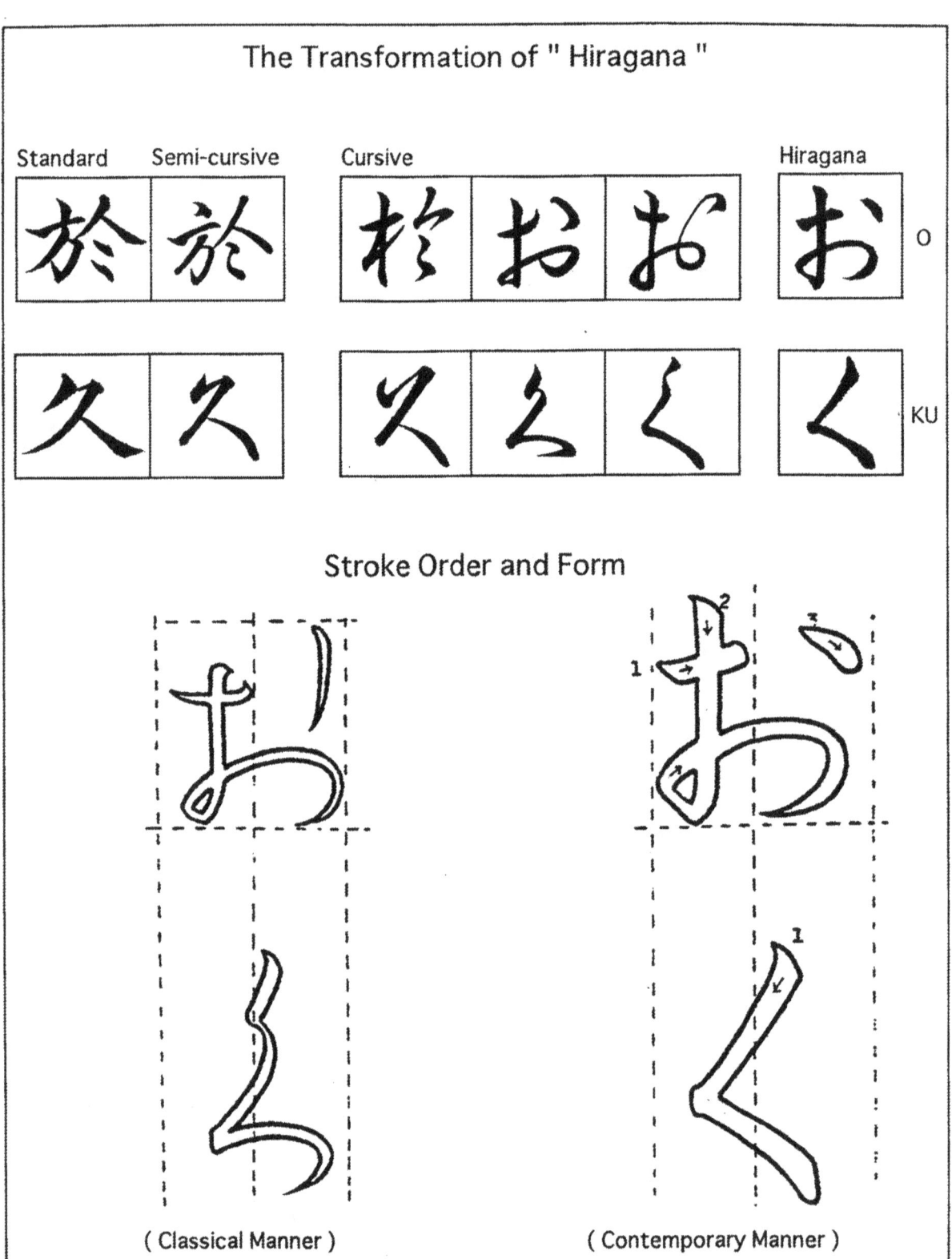

Standard　Semi-cursive　　　Cursive　　　　　　　　　Hiragana

於　於　　　於　お　お　　お　O

久　久　　　久　ろ　く　　く　KU

Stroke Order and Form

(Classical Manner)　　　　　　　(Contemporary Manner)

The Transformation of " Hiragana "

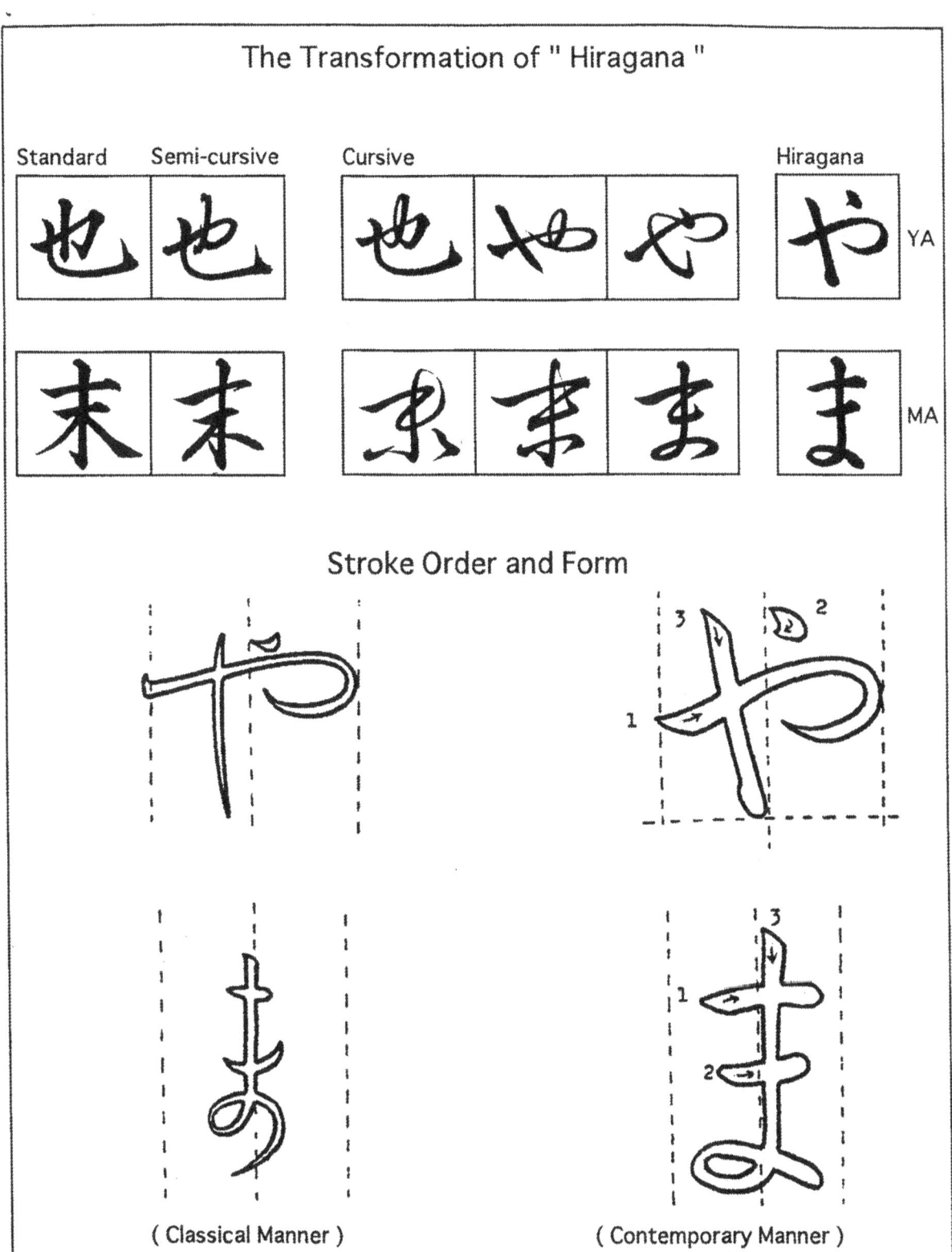

Standard   Semi-cursive   Cursive   Hiragana

也   也   也   や   や   や   YA

末   末   末   末   ま   ま   MA

Stroke Order and Form

(Classical Manner)   (Contemporary Manner)

The Transformation of " Hiragana "

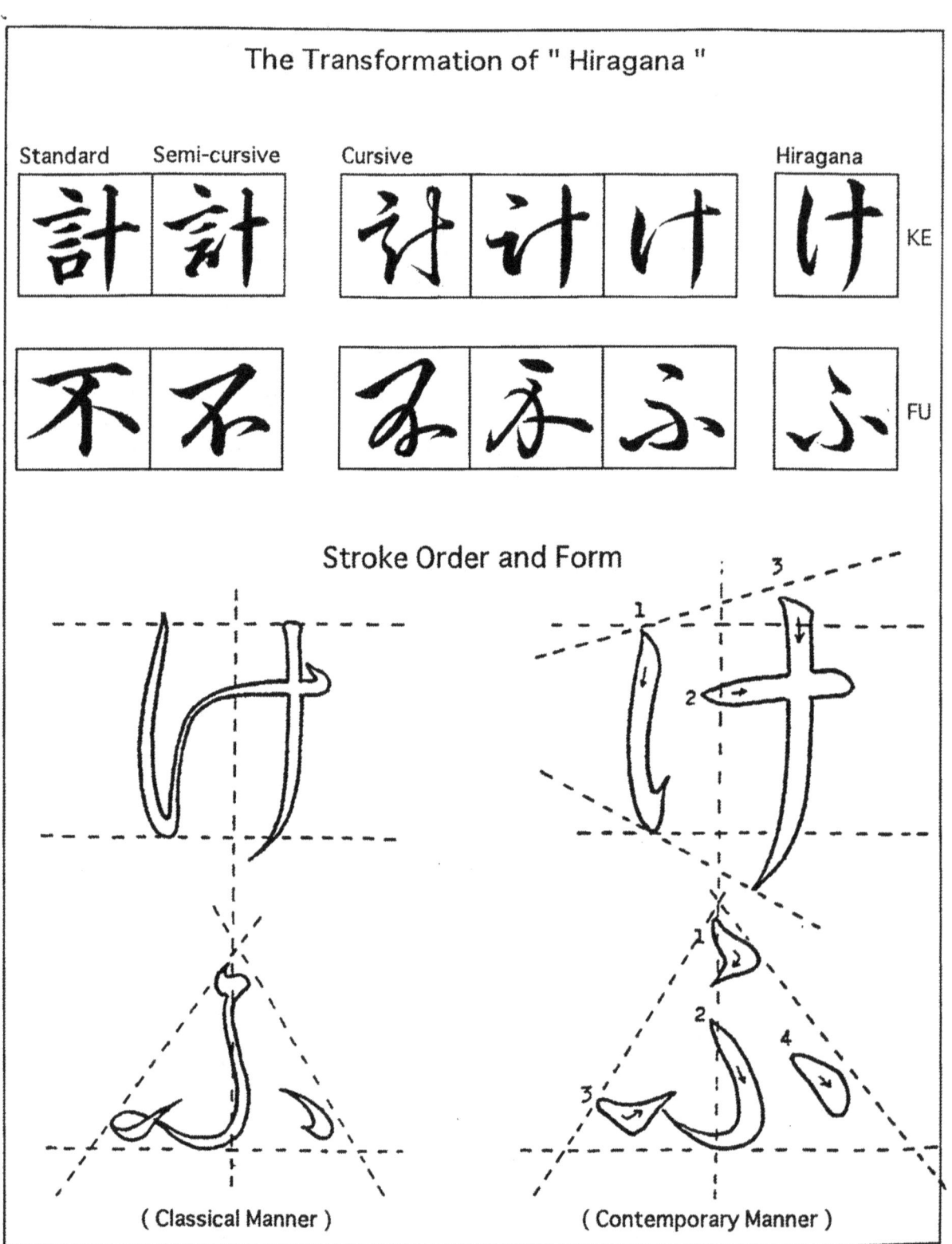

Standard	Semi-cursive	Cursive			Hiragana	
計	計	計	計	け	け	KE
不	不	不	禾	ふ	ふ	FU

Stroke Order and Form

(Classical Manner)   (Contemporary Manner)

The Transformation of " Hiragana "

Standard	Semi-cursive	Cursive			Hiragana	
己	乙	己	?	て	こ	KO
衣	衣	衣	元	?	え	E

Stroke Order and Form

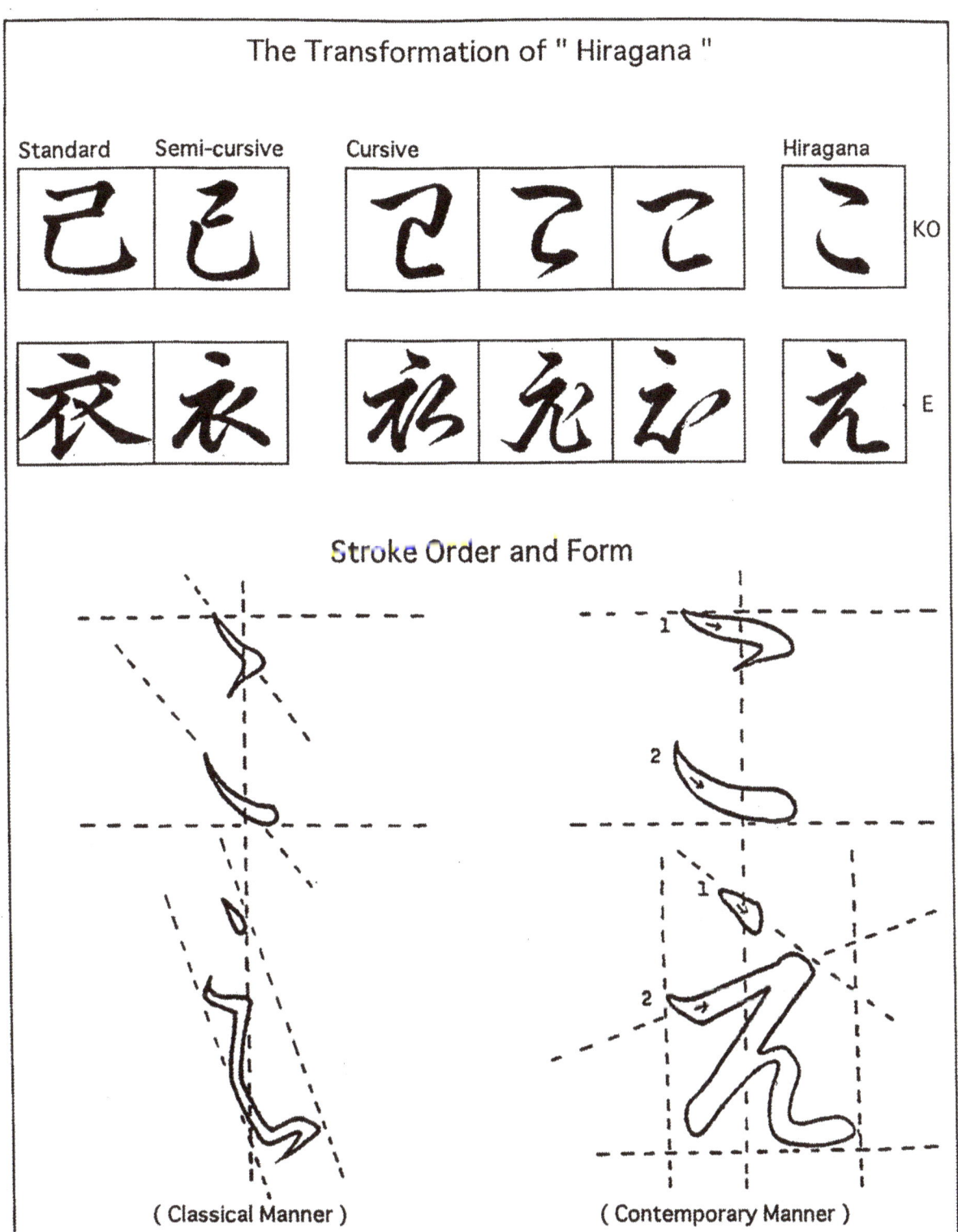

(Classical Manner)   (Contemporary Manner)

The Transformation of " Hiragana "

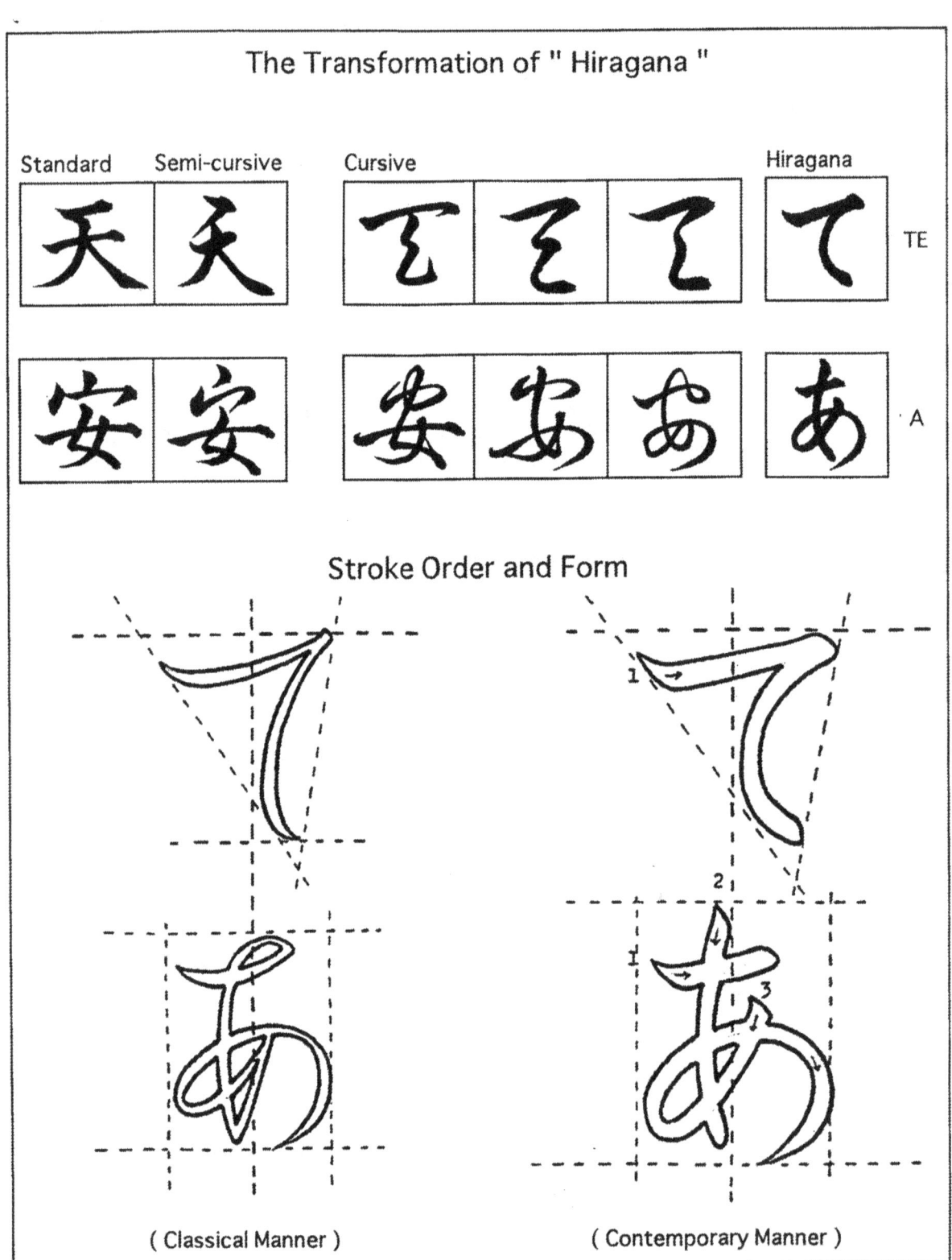

Standard   Semi-cursive   Cursive   Hiragana

天 天   乙 そ て   て   TE

安 安   安 あ あ   あ   A

Stroke Order and Form

(Classical Manner)   (Contemporary Manner)

The Transformation of " Hiragana "

Standard	Semi-cursive	Cursive			Hiragana	
左	左	圭	左	ち	さ	SA
幾	幾	糸	幾	き	き	KI

Stroke Order and Form

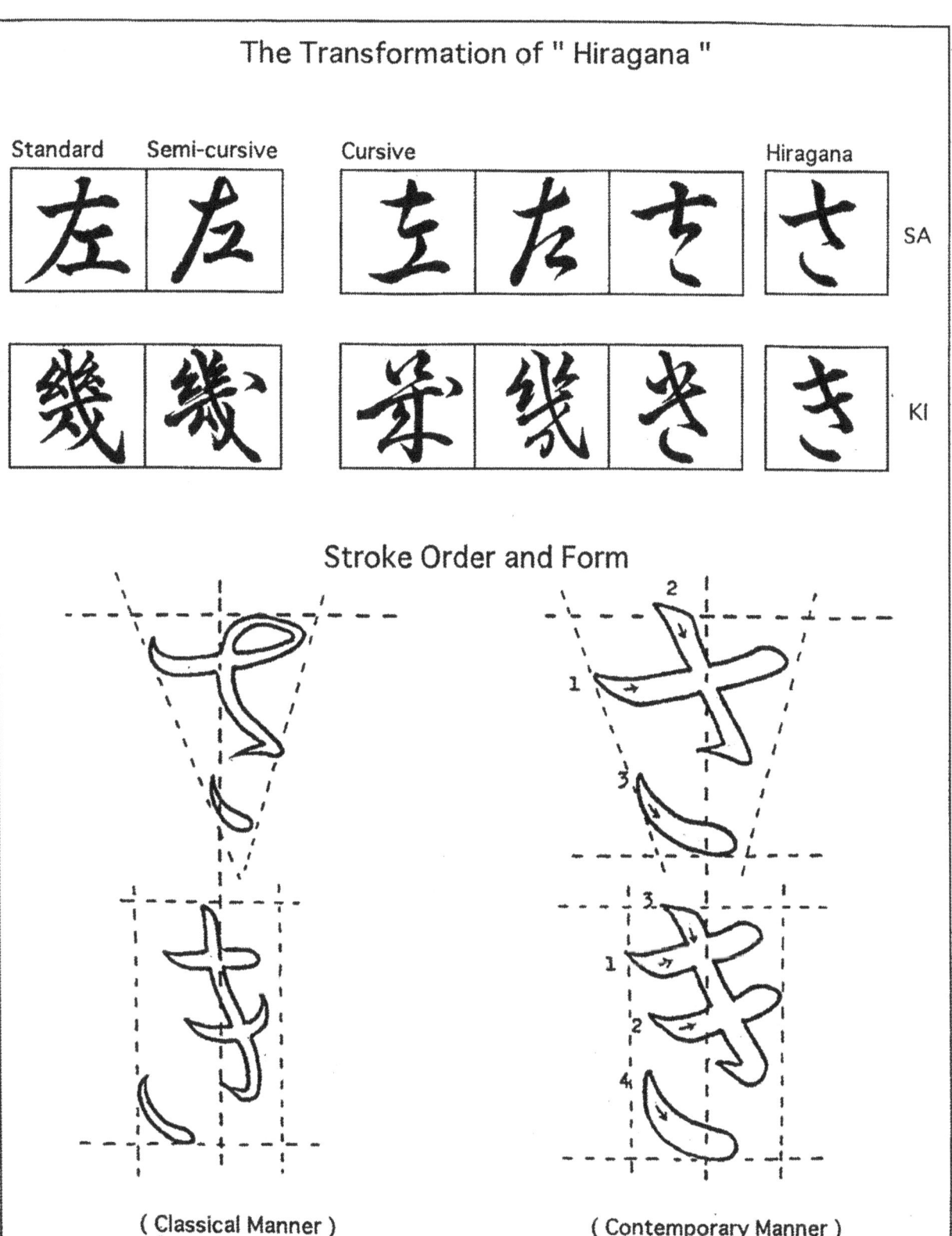

(Classical Manner)   (Contemporary Manner)

33

The Transformation of " Hiragana "

Standard	Semi-cursive	Cursive			Hiragana	
由	由	𢑑	由	ゆ	ゆ	YU
女	女	女	女	め	め	ME

Stroke Order and Form

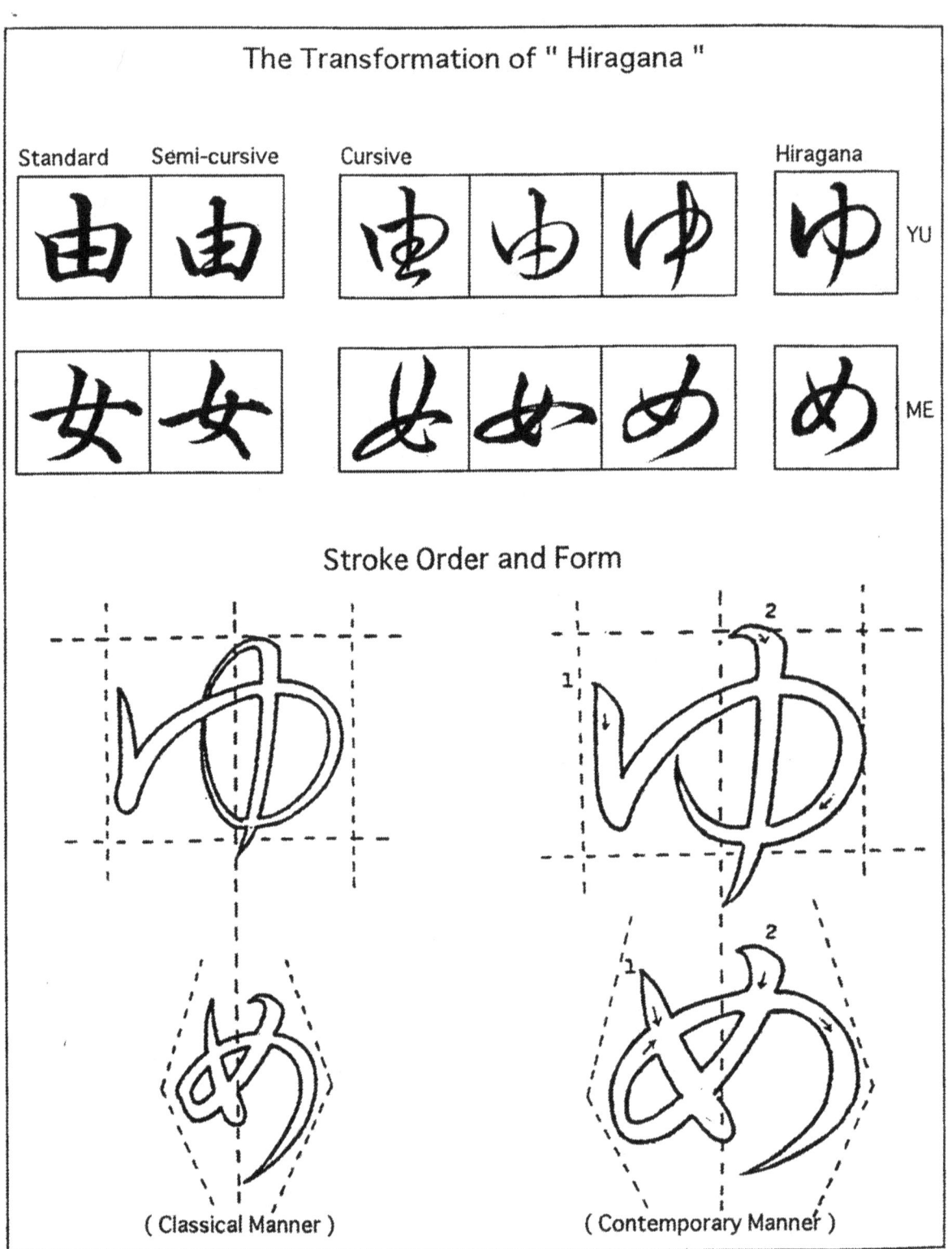

(Classical Manner)　　　　　　(Contemporary Manner)

The Transformation of " Hiragana "

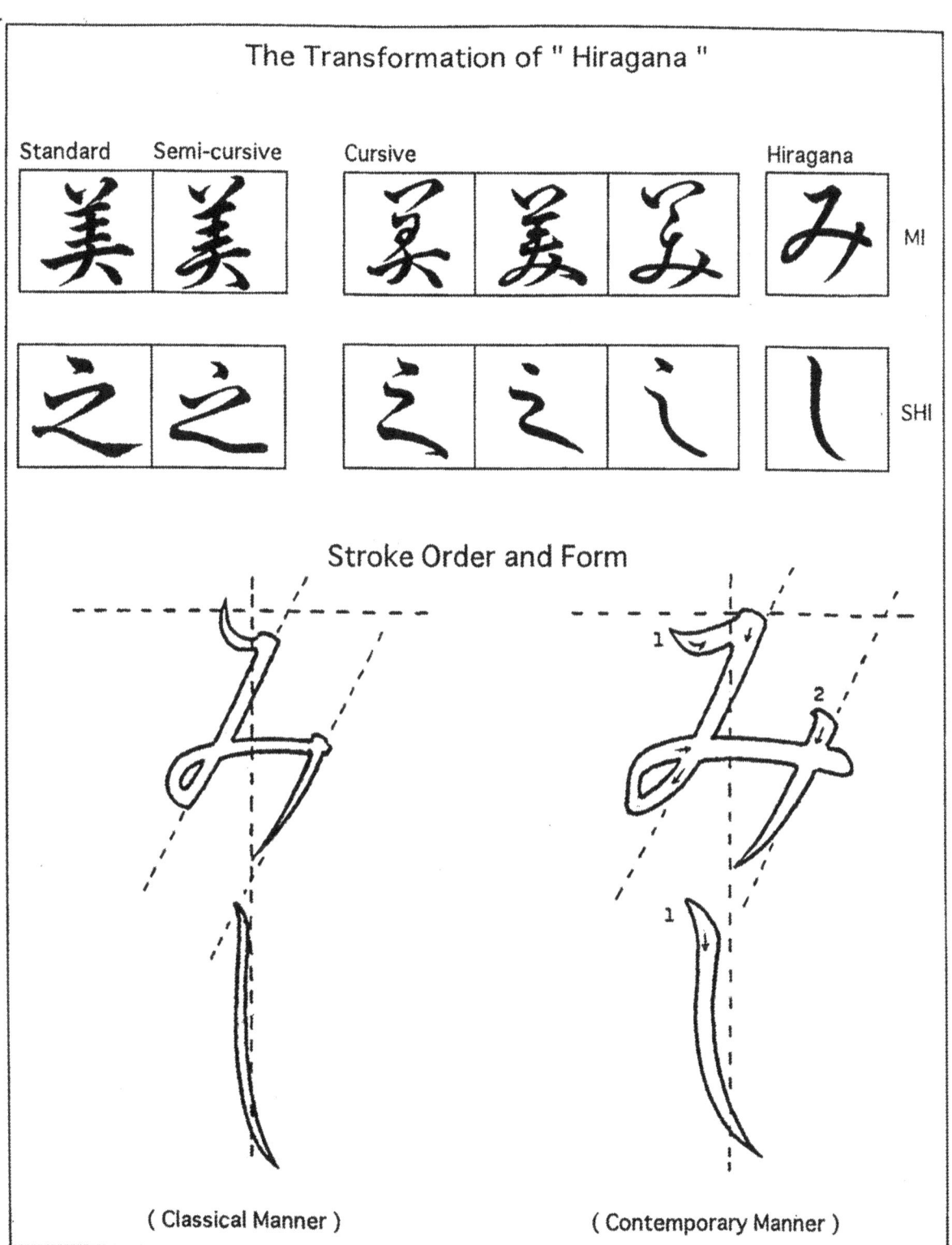

Standard | Semi-cursive | Cursive | Hiragana

美 美 | 羙 羙 羙 | み   MI

之 之 | 之 之 之 | し   SHI

Stroke Order and Form

(Classical Manner)   (Contemporary Manner)

The Transformation of " Hiragana "

Standard	Semi-cursive	Cursive			Hiragana	
恵	恵	恵	𠌫	𠌫	ゑ	E
比	比	比	比	ひ	ひ	HI

Stroke Order and Form

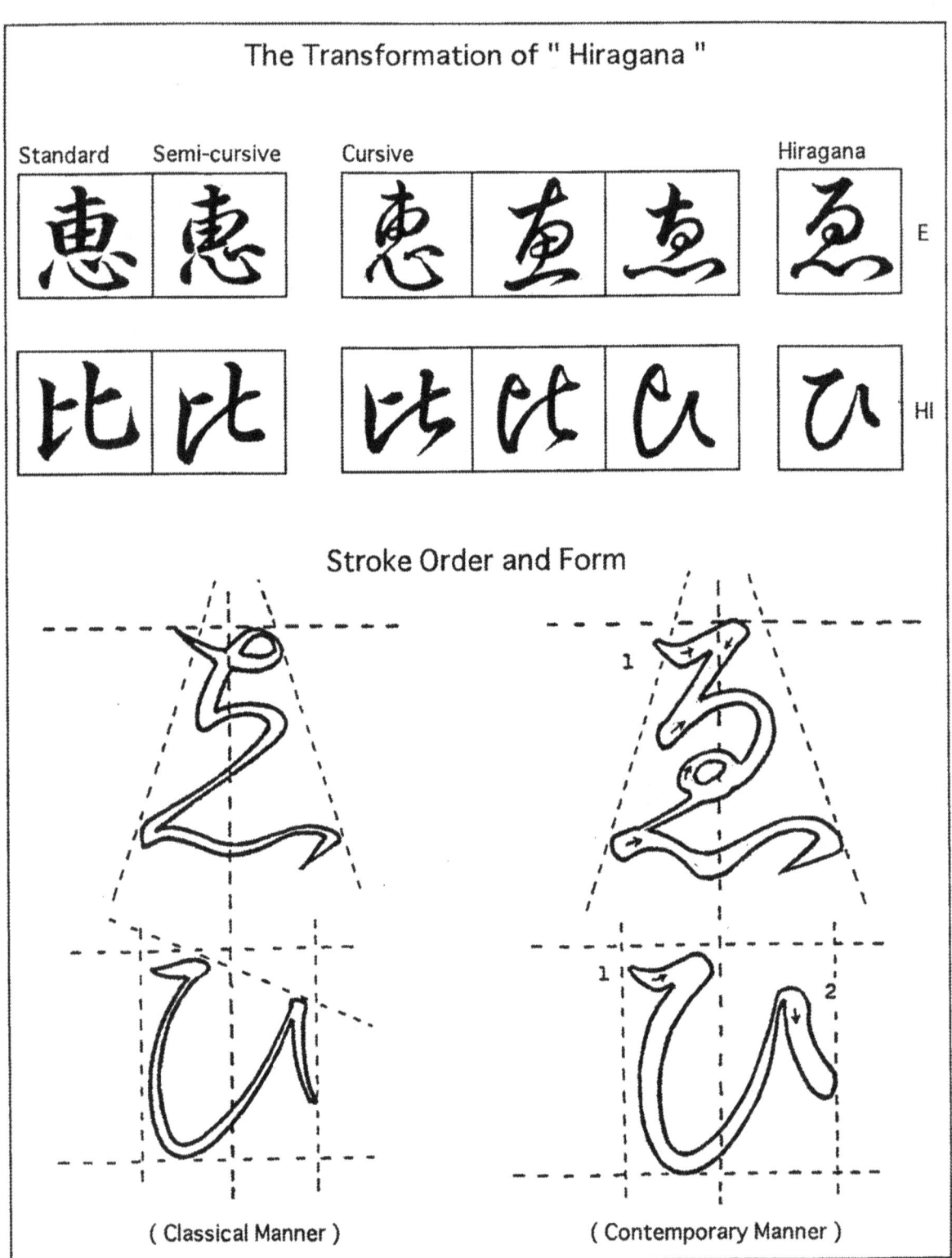

(Classical Manner)   (Contemporary Manner)

The Transformation of " Hiragana "

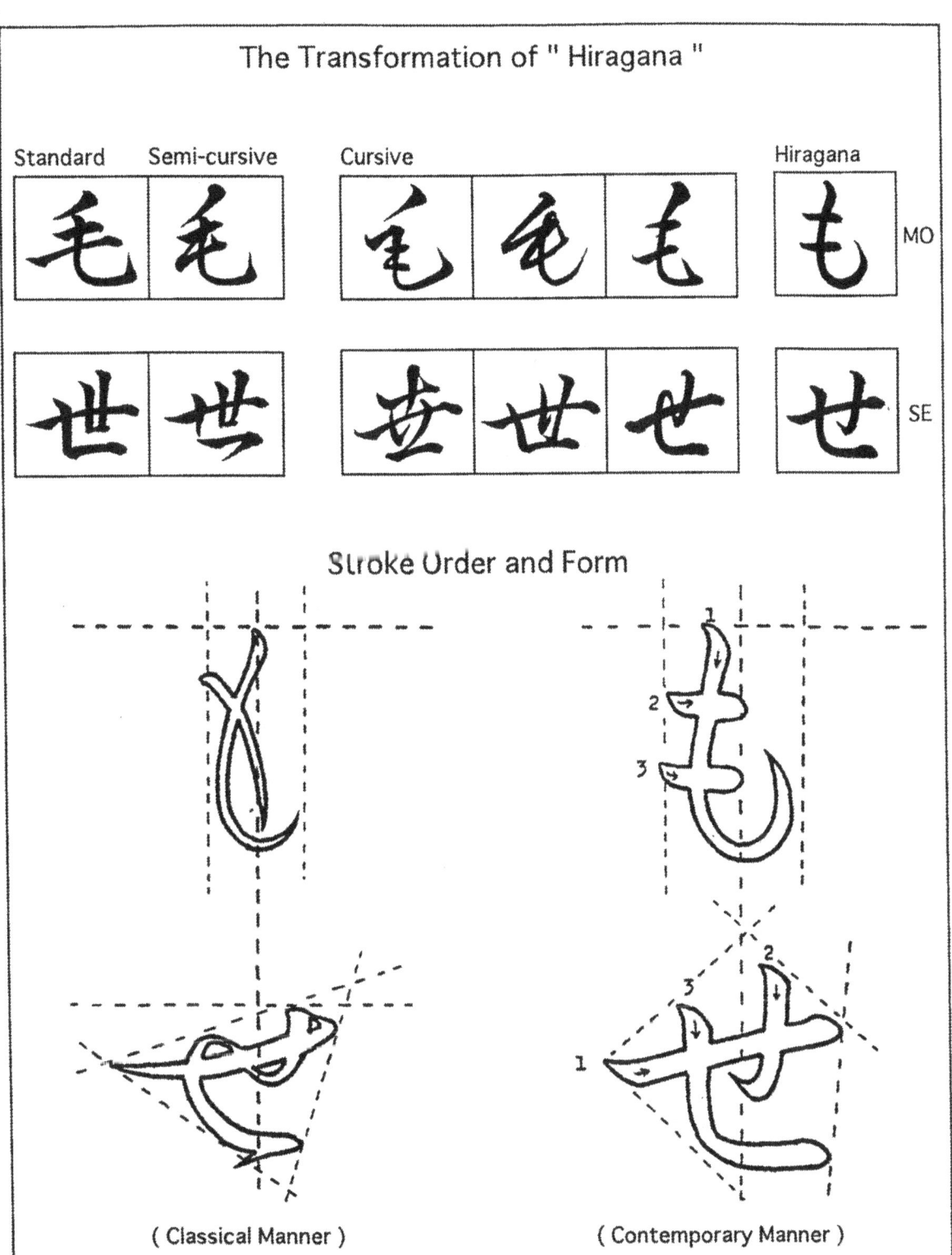

Standard	Semi-cursive		Cursive			Hiragana	
毛	毛		毛	毛	毛	も	MO
世	世		世	世	世	せ	SE

Stroke Order and Form

(Classical Manner)　　　　　(Contemporary Manner)

The Transformation of " Hiragana "

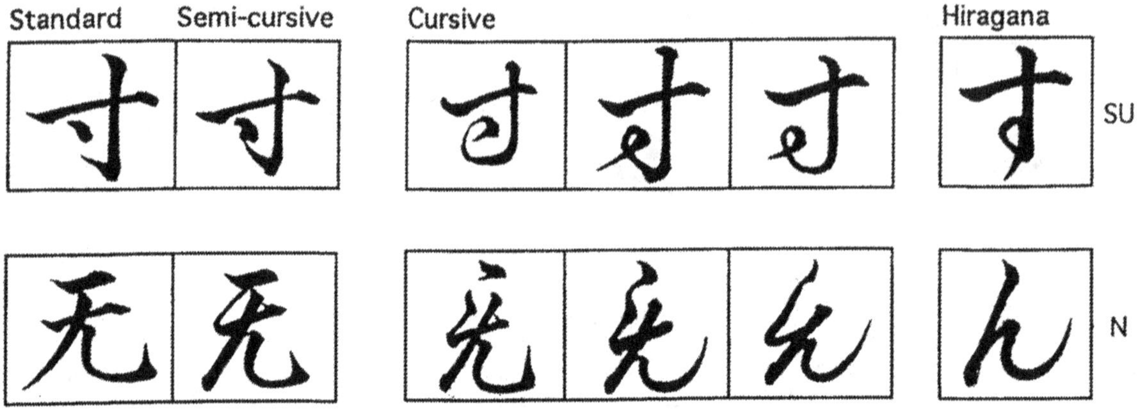

Standard
Semi-cursive
Cursive
Hiragana
SU
N

Stroke Order and Form

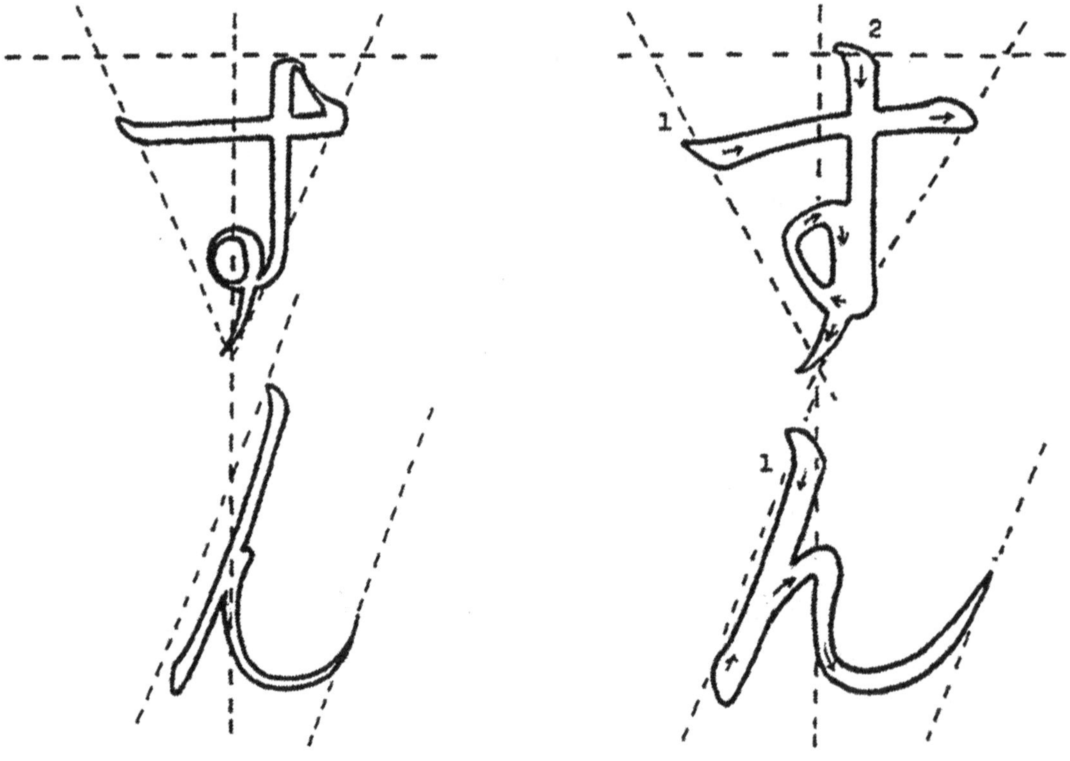

2
1
1

(Classical Manner) (Contemporary Manner)

Japanese Characters 日本の文字 are the following five different kinds of characters.

   1) Kanji (Chinese characters)
   2) Hiragana (A phonetic syllabary)
   3) Katakana (A phonetic syllabary)
   4) Romaji (Roman alphabet)
   5) Arabic numerals

1) Kanji 漢字 (Chinese characters)

Kanji characters represent meaning. One Kanji character often has one or more readings (pronunciations) and meanings. Kanji characters originated in ancient China and were introduced into Japan around the 4th or 5th century A.D.. Officially, Chinese priests brought thousands of Chinese books (sutras and related with Buddhism) to Japan in 538, or 552 A.D.. This is the first public arrival of Kanji Characters in Japan.

   ex.   安 AN, peace, calm; yasu(i) cheap; -yasu(i) easy to
        山 SAN, yama mountain

2) Hiragana 平仮名 (A phonetic syllabary)

A Hiragana phonetic alphabet was invented from the cursive style of a Chinese Character in the beginning of the Heian period (794 - 1185)

   ex.   あき AKI, autumn
        はな HANA, flower

3) Katakana 片仮名 (A phonetic syllabary)

A Katakana phonetic alphabet was simplified and was made from a half or part of a Kanji (Chinese character) during the Heian period. Katakana is used primarily for foreign names, place names and words of foreign origin.

   ex.   サン・フランシスコ SAN-FRANCISCO, San Francisco
        シスコ SHISUKO, S.F.

4) Romaji (Roman alphabet)

Romaji is used only in limited cases such as : Name of persons, road signs, station signs and abbreviations of foreign languages.

   ex.   TOKYO, YOKOHAMA, HANEDA, UEDA, HANAKO-HAYASHI, TEL, telephone

5) Arabic numerals

Arabic numerals are always used for scientific formulas.

   ex. $10 + 6 = 16$ $12 - 6 = 6$

The Number of Kanji (Chinese Characters) 漢字の数

The oldest Chinese dictionary named Setsumonkaiji 説文解字 (The Etymology and the Analysis of the Chinese Language), was compiled by Kyoshin 許慎 (Hsushen) in 122 A.D.. This dictionary was 9353 characters. The number of Kanji contained in the old dictionary "Koki-jiten 康煕字典 (The Imperial Dictionary)" reached to more than 40,000 Kanji Characters. This dictionary compiled by Cho-gyoku-sho 張玉書 (Chang-hsueh-shu) and Chin-tei-kei 陳廷敬 (Chong-ting-ching) in 1710 A.D.. However, only 3000 to 5000 Kanji characters are used in daily life in Japan. In 1946, the Japanese Ministry of Education established a special selection of 1850 Kanji characters for daily use (Toyo-Kanji 当用漢字). At the same time, the government selected 881 Kanji characters as the Kyoiku-Kanji 教育漢字 (the Educational Kanji) which should be studied within the period of elementary education 1 - 6 grade). In 1981, the government reorganized the number of Kanji characters, and as a result, acquired 1945 Kanji characters for daily use (Joyo-Kanji 常用漢字) and 996 Kanji characters (Kyoikuyo-Kanji 教育用漢字) for the Educational Kanji Characters.

The Reading of Kanji - On 音 and Kun 訓

One Kanji can express one meaning and carry one Chinese pronunciation. The On-reading is the pronunciation based on the Chinese sound which is partly Japanized. For instance, (山) is read "san" in On-reading in accordance with the Chinese sound "shan". The native Japanese pronunciation, applied to the Kanji according to the meaning, is so- called Kun-reading. For example, (山) is read "yama" in the Kun-reading, following the native word which means "a mountain". The Kun reading is the translation from Chinese to Japanese.

Forms of Japanese Old Rhythmed Verses for Japanese Calligraphy

*Waka (和歌) : a Japanese ode (=poem)

> 1) Tanka (短歌) : a Tanka-poem
> 2) Choka (長歌) : a Long poem
> 3) Sedoka (施頭歌) : a Sedoka-poem, a Repetitive poem
> 4) Renga (連歌) : a Role-poem, a Two-person poem, a Chain-poem
> 5) Haiku (俳句) : a Haiku-poem
> 6) Senryu (川柳) : a Senryu-poem, a Satire poem

* Except above listed Japanese old rhythmed verses, Kanshi (漢詩) : Chinese poems, especially Toshi (唐詩) : Tung poems were written by famous and well-educated people in Japan for such a long period, from 6th century to the present.

1) Tanka :   A Tanka-poem contains thirty-one syllables such as the 5.7.5.7.7 syllable form.

2) Choka :   A Japanese long poem is formed by the 5.7.5.7....5.7.7 syllable form.

3) Sedoka :   A Sedoka-poem is composed by 5.7.7.5.7.7....... syllables.

4) Renga :   A Role-poem is built up by the first half of a Tanka-poem (5.7.5. syllables) and the lower hemistich (7.7 syllables). One makes the first half of a Tanka-poem, then another completes the lower hemistich of a poem. Many people took up a Renga-poem during the Muromachi period (1392 - 1573).

5) Haiku :   A Haiku-poem is constituted by seventeen syllables and the 5.7.5 syllable form. When making a Haiku-poem, you need a seasonal word. If you drop a seasonal word, your poem becomes a Senryu poem. A Haiku-poem was independent of the first half of a Tanka-poem (5.7.5 syllables). Poet Basho Matsuo (1644 - 1694) and Poet Buson Yosa (1716 - 1783) established beautiful Haiku-poems as an art during the Edo period (1603 - 1868). The word of Haiku, 'Hai' means "to make a joke" and "ku" has a meaning of "a phrase or a poem".

6) Senryu :   A Senryu-poem has the same syllable form as the Haiku. No need to have a seasonal word in a poem. Senryu was very popular during the Edo period. Secret words and slang were often employed among lovers and business people in their Senryu poems. Japanese contemporary literary people are still researching the meaning of Senryu poems. Senryu is a satire poem.

Matsuo, Basho (松尾芭蕉 1644 - 1694), Haiku poet

Among the Japanese literary works, Basho's Haiku poem "Furuikeya....." has the highest frequency of being translated into English.

The total number of the different English translations of "Furuikeya..." already reached 100. This is an unbelievable experience. The following poem is the Basho's completed "Furuikeya...." Haiku poem with two examples of the translation.

*In the season of spring

Fu - ru - i - ke - ya
ふるいけや
Ka - wa - zu - to - bi - ko - mu
かわつとひこむ
Mi - zu - no - o - to
みつのおと

ex. 1

Old pond - frogs - jumped in
                sound of water

                tr. by Lafcadio Hern (1850 - 1904)
                (Koizumi, Yagumo)

ex. 2

The ancient pond
A frog leaps in
The sound of the water
                tr. by Donald Keene
                (Japanologist)

The Origin of Haiku

Students, notice the diagram I drew for you.
The diagram indicates the various sources of spiritual concepts.
The relation of oriental thoughts regarding Haiku is the following:

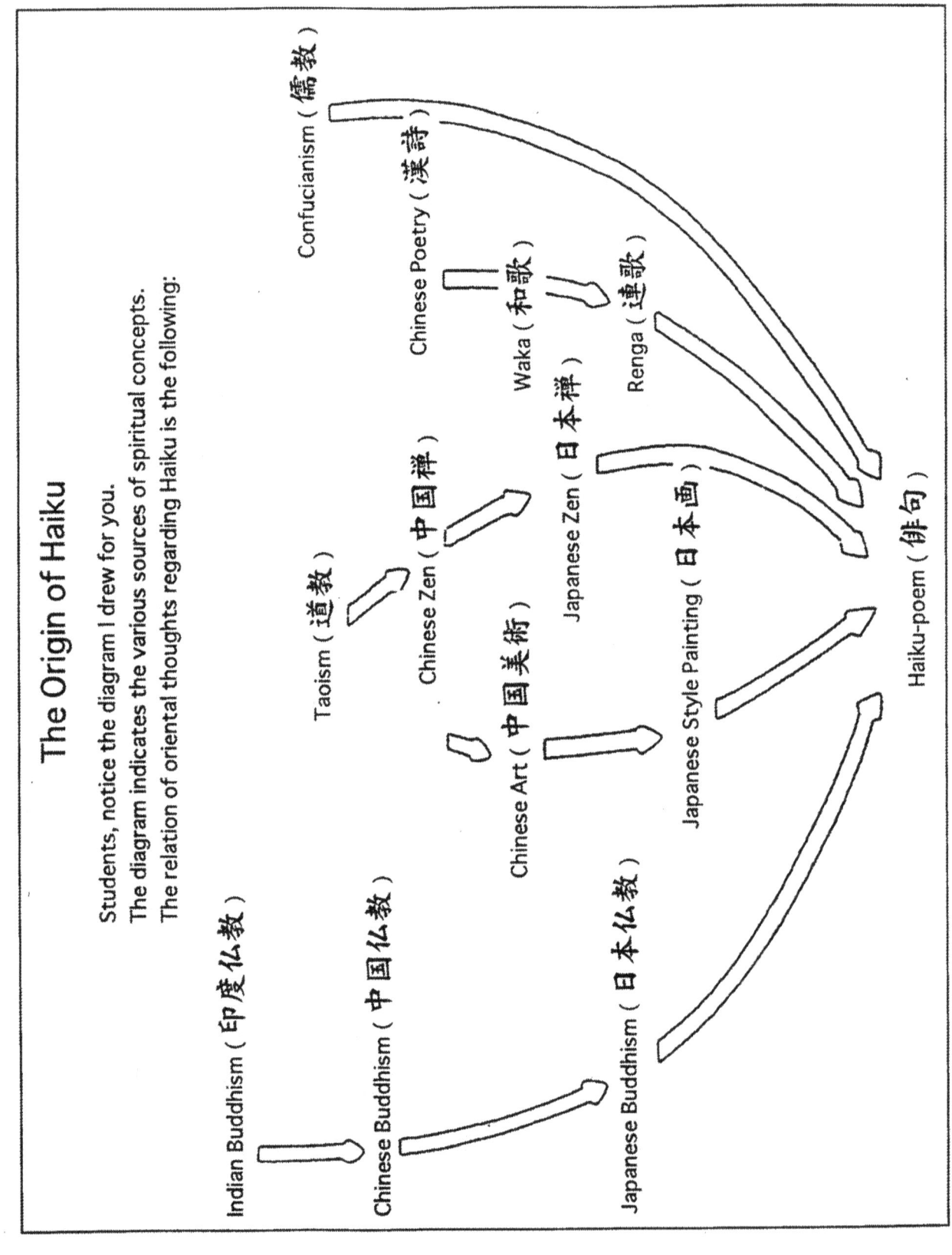

Indian Buddhism (印度仏教)

Chinese Buddhism (中国仏教)

Japanese Buddhism (日本仏教)

Confucianism (儒教)

Chinese Poetry (漢詩)

Waka (和歌)

Renga (連歌)

Taoism (道教)

Chinese Zen (中国禅)

Japanese Zen (日本禅)

Chinese Art (中国美術)

Japanese Style Painting (日本画)

Haiku-poem (俳句)

Renmen　連綿　(the Continuous Stroke)

1) Tantai 単体 (the single character writing)　　ex.　い i
　　　　　　　　　　　　　　　　　　　　　　　　　ろ ro
　　　　　　　　　　　　　　　　　　　　　　　　　は ha

2) Renmen 連綿 (the continuous stroke)　ex.　い i
　　　　　　　　　　　　　　　　　　　　　ろ ro
　　　　　　　　　　　　　　　　　　　　　は ha

a) Niji-renmen　　二字連綿 (Two character continuous stroke)

b) Sanji-renmen　三字連綿 (Three character continuous stroke)

c) Yoji-renmen　　四字連綿 (Four character continuous stroke)

d) Goji-renmen　　五字連綿 (Five character continuous stroke)

ex.

a)　ha
　　ru

haru (spring)

b)　ha
　　ru
　　ni

haruni (in spring)

c)　ha
　　ru
　　ka
　　ze

harukaze (spring wind)

d)　ha
　　ru
　　no
　　u
　　ta

harunouta (spring song)

A) Gyo-gaki　　行書き (the Gyo (Space out) Writing)

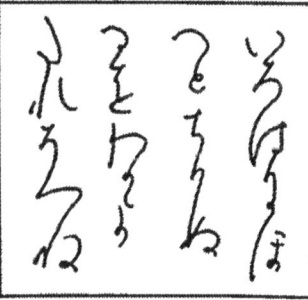

B) Chirashi-gaki 散らし書き (the Scattering Writing)

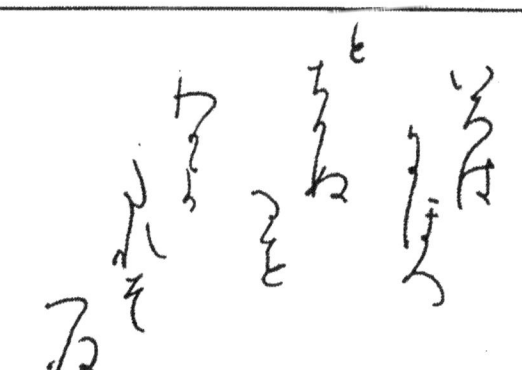

Part of a Poem (The I-RO-HA UTA, p2)

Koya-gire (高野切), attributes Kino Tsurayuki (紀貫之 ? - 946)

The meaning of the word "Koya-gire" means: "Koya" is the name of the temple "Mt. Koya" in Wakayama prefecture. "-gire" has a meaning of "piece or part". Koya-gire is the section of an incomplete transcription of kokinshu (古今集 905). Mt. Koya temple used to own Koya-gire. The name of "Koya-gire" was derived from the part of a collection of Mt. Koya temple. But originally, Koya-gire was the property of Konoe Family (近衛家). At the beginning, there were 20 volumes. But now only 9 volumes remain. Koya-gire has three kinds of calligraphic writing styles, called Koya-gire isshu (高野切一種), Koya-gire nishu (高野切二種) and Koya-gire sanshu (高野切三種). This means, possibly three different calligraphers wrote these volumes. We speculate that these calligraphers duplicated Kino Tsurayuki's original copies. The following examples are from the part of Koya-gire isshu.

ex. "Haru は る , は 留 " has a meaning of "spring".

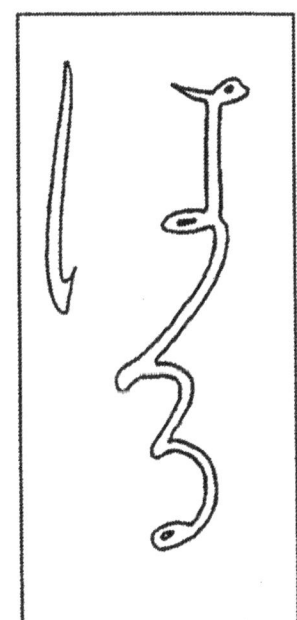
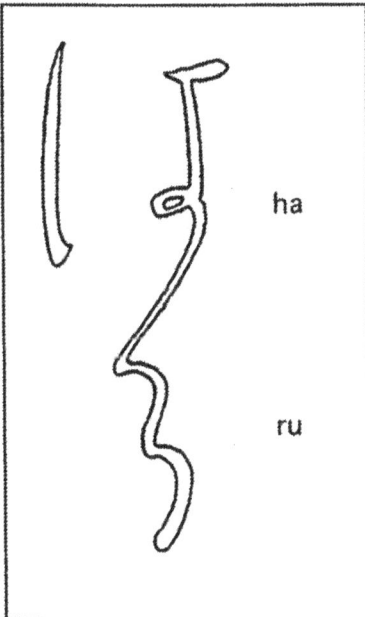
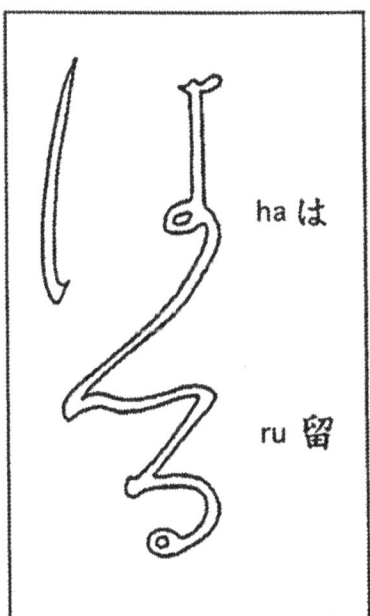

Sanjikishi (三色紙 Three sets of joined shikishi)

1) Sunshoan Shikishi (寸松庵色紙) 10c A.D.
Ki no Tsurayuki (紀貫之) ? - 946

This Kana-calligraphy art work was a part of General Sakuma, who was well-known as a tea ceremony master. This calligraphy was called "Sunshoan" after the name of General Sakuma, Masakatsu's tea house. The tea house was located in Daitoku-ji (Temple), Shino in Kyoto. Small pine trees were planted in front of the tea house. In the early stage, this calligraphy album consisted of 36 leaves. General Sakuma, Masakatsu owned 12 leaves of Kana-calligraphy, but now different owners own these 36 leaves calligraphy separately. This calligraphy used to be very famous calligraphy as Tsurayuki, Kino's work. Unfortunately, there is no reliable documents which survived.

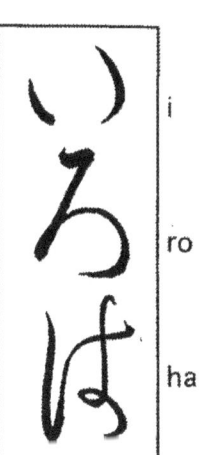

i

ro

ha

2) Tsugi-jikishi (継色紙) 10c A.D.
Ono no Michikaze (Tofu) (小野道風) 894 - 966

Tsugi-jikishi indicates a paper form of a written Tanka-poem in shikishi paper (square rice paper), jointed two square rice papers. Tsugi means "to joint". This is the reason that people call this paper form "Tsugi-shikishi" or "Tsugi-jikishi". Originally Tsugi-jikishi was an album. In 1906 (39th year of Meiji Era), calligraphy collectors divided this album into one poem each. This calligraphy is extremely beautiful art work, with clean and deep line quality, the transformation of the ink color is naturally expressed. Tsugi-jikishi calligraphy was handed down as Ono no Michikaze's work for a long time. Unfortunately, Tsugi-jikishi is not backed up by documentation, but by legend.

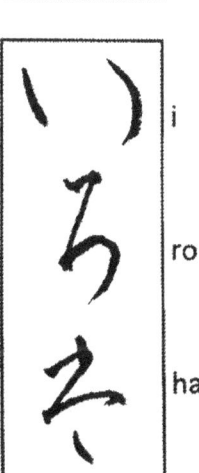

i

ro

ha

3) Masu-jikishi (升色紙) 11c A.D.
Fujiwara, Yukinari (藤原行成) 972 - 1027

Masu-jikishi calligraphy handed down a long time ago. But there is no documentation available today. This calligraphy looks very skillful and is a well-expressed movement of flowing lines by comparison with two other Shikishi-calligraphy. At an early stage, Masu-jikishi was written in form of an album, not in shikishi-size paper. Originally Masu-jikishi was an album, but posterity collectors chopped this album leaves and remounted it in square shaped rice paper.

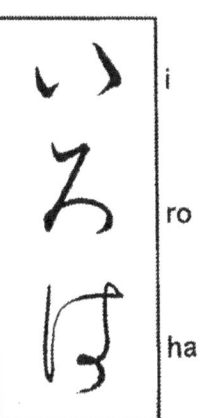

i

ro

ha

The Sesonji Style of Calligraphy (世尊寺流)
Fujiwara, Yukinari (藤原行成 972 - 1027)

Fujiwara, Yukinari, he developed "The Sesonji Style (世尊寺流) of calligraphy", so called the Sesonji style of writing derived from the Ono no Michikaze (894 - 966)'s manner of writing. This Sesonji style of writing became very popular during the end of the Heian period and also at the beginning of the Kamakura period (1185 - 1392). Everyone adopted this style calligraphy, not just the courts and leading factions of the country, but also the total populace took a real liking to the smooth and refined style of Fujiwara, Yukinari, it really expressed the character of Fujiwara, Yukinari. All of his work was a major happening in the Heian period, one compared the appearance of his work like people playing a game in colorful autumn field. An interesting book on the subject of calligraphy is "Judokusho 入木抄", Prince Sonen (尊円親王 1298 - 1356) who edited this book concentrated on his criticism of Fujiwara, Yukinari's manner of calligraphy.

ya
ma
za
ku
ra

* Masu-jikishi (升色紙) 11c A.D.

Yamazakura (山桜) a wild cherry tree

EQUIPMENT　用具

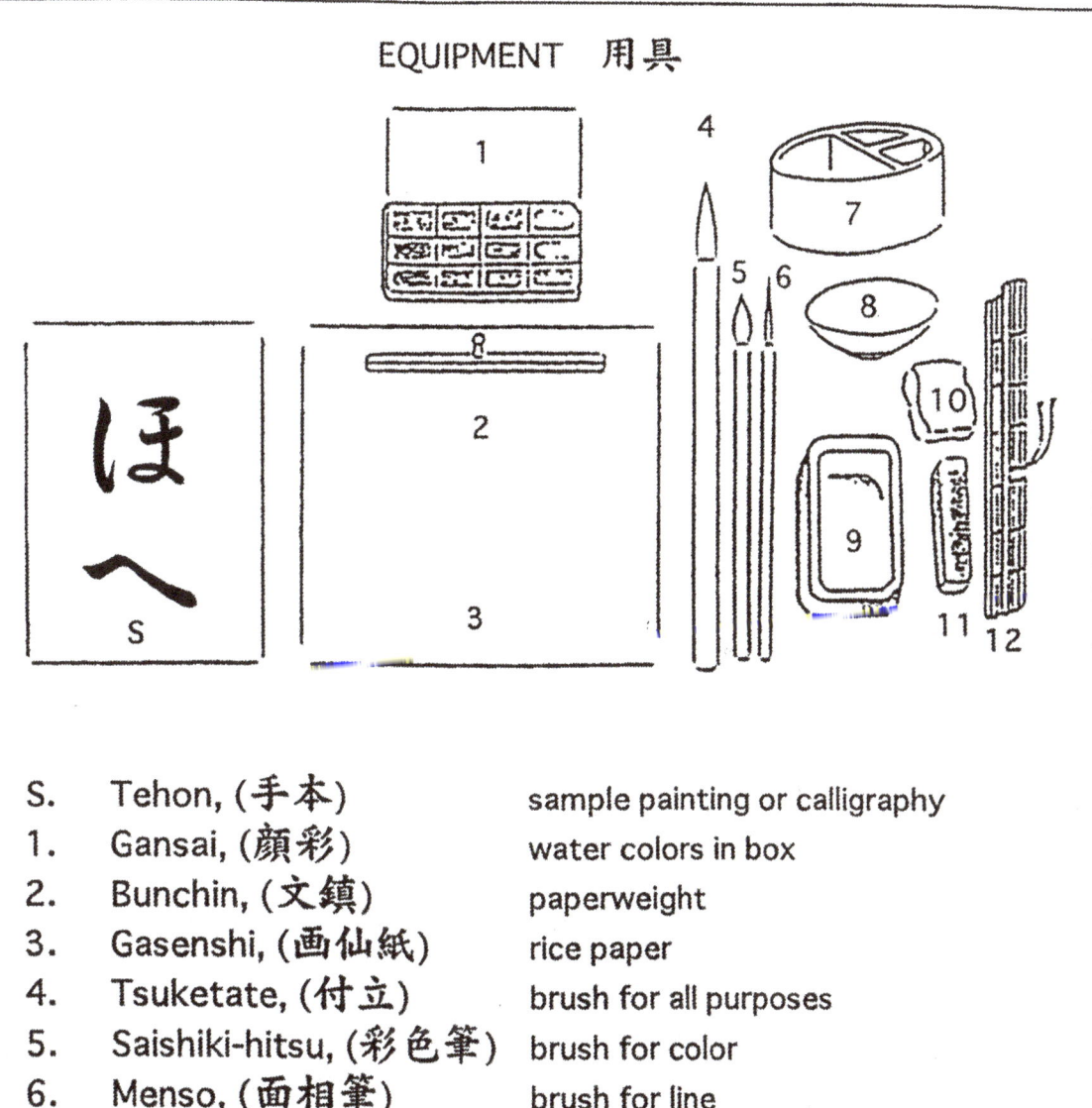

S.	Tehon, (手本)	sample painting or calligraphy
1.	Gansai, (顔彩)	water colors in box
2.	Bunchin, (文鎮)	paperweight
3.	Gasenshi, (画仙紙)	rice paper
4.	Tsuketate, (付立)	brush for all purposes
5.	Saishiki-hitsu, (彩色筆)	brush for color
6.	Menso, (面相筆)	brush for line
7.	Hissen, (筆洗)	water container for cleaning brushes
8.	Enoguzara, (絵具皿)	flat dish used as palette
9.	Suzuri, (硯)	stone for rubbing ink
10.	Nuno, (布)	cloth
11.	Sumi, (墨)	ink stick
12.	Fude-maki, (筆巻き)	bamboo container for brushes

The names of each part of an inkstone

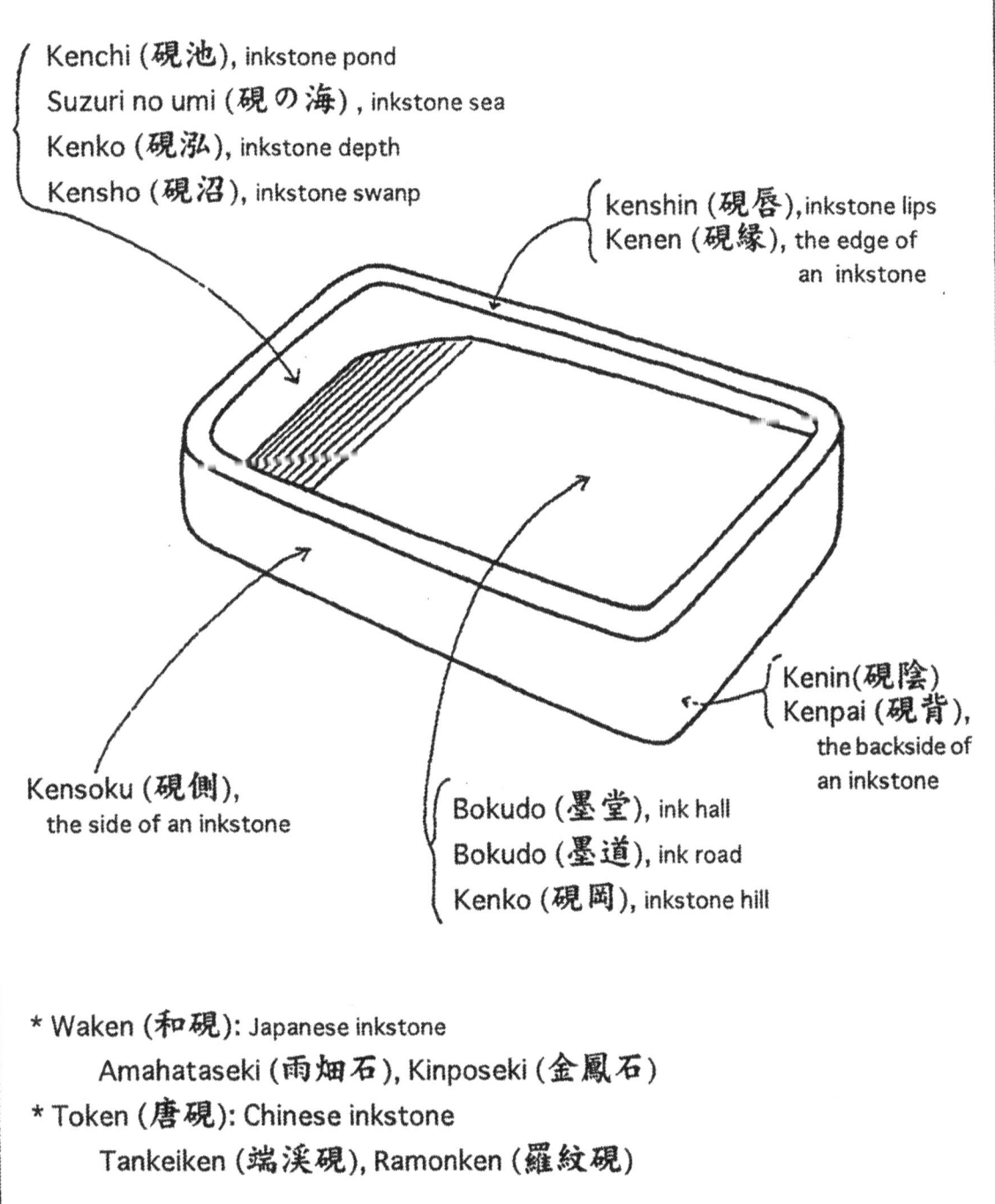

Kenchi (硯池), inkstone pond
Suzuri no umi (硯の海), inkstone sea
Kenko (硯泓), inkstone depth
Kensho (硯沼), inkstone swanp

kenshin (硯唇), inkstone lips
Kenen (硯縁), the edge of an inkstone

Kenin(硯陰)
Kenpai (硯背),
the backside of an inkstone

Kensoku (硯側),
the side of an inkstone

Bokudo (墨堂), ink hall
Bokudo (墨道), ink road
Kenko (硯岡), inkstone hill

* Waken (和硯): Japanese inkstone
　　Amahataseki (雨畑石), Kinposeki (金鳳石)
* Token (唐硯): Chinese inkstone
　　Tankeiken (端渓硯), Ramonken (羅紋硯)

1) How to hold a brush　（筆の持ち方）

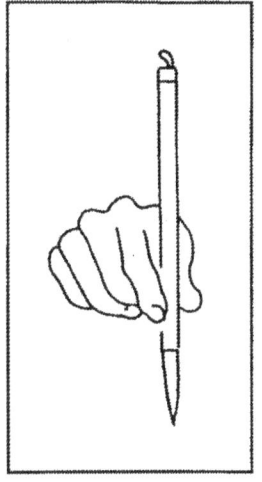
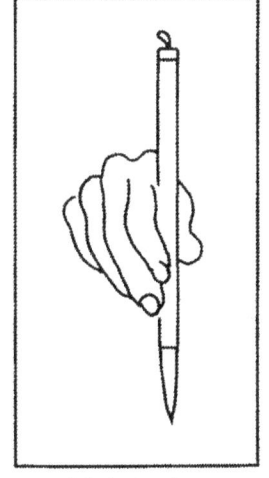

A) Tanko-ho

B) Soko-ho

A) Tanko-ho（単鉤法）

is writing small characters.

B) Soko-ho（双鉤法）

is writing still larger characters.

2) The position of the wrist　（腕の位置）

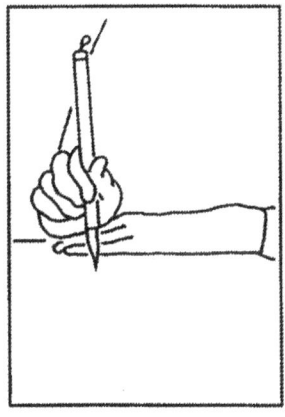
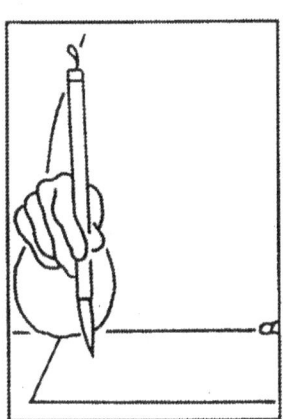
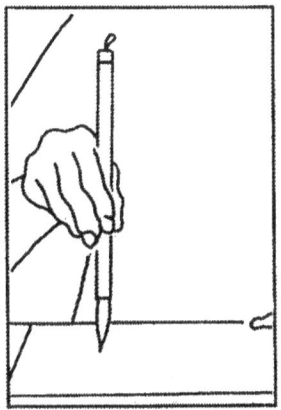

a) Chinwan-ho

b) Teiwan-ho

c) Kenwan-ho

a) Chinwan-ho（枕腕法）, This method is most convenient for writing small characters, pillow wrist.

b) Teiwan-ho（提腕法）, is for still larger characters, both wrist and elbow are held above the table.

c) Kenwan-ho（懸腕法）, suspended wrist, is without doubt it is the most important position in training of a calligrapher.

The Meaning of "Shodo, Shuji, Tenarai"

I) Shodo (書道)

"Shodo" is the art to aim to write characters beautifully with a brush.

II)Shuji (習字)

"Shuji" means to learn how to write characters.

III) Tenarai (手習い)

"Tenarai" means to practice to write characters.

How to practice writing characters with a brush

1) Rinsho (臨書)

"Rinsho" means to practice to write characters looking at the sample calligraphy. Then, usually the sample calligraphy should be put the left side of your practicing rice paper.

2)Mosho (模書)

"Mosho" is a tracing manner. At first, you put the thin and transparent paper on top of the sample calligraphy. Then trace the shape of the character.

3) Ansho (暗書)

"Ansho" means to write characters which you have been practicing with a brush, without looking at the sample calligraphy.

4) Hosho (倣書)

Originally, Hosho means to imitate to write characters.

For example, if you practice the character " 口 kuchi, mouth", you could also write a simillar character " 呂 ro, backbone".

5) Jiun (自運)

"Jiun" means to write characters with a brush freely using your skill that you have been practicing in calligraphical manner, without looking at the sample calligraphy on the left side.

6 Types of Calligraphy (六体 Rikutai)

Kumo

雲
く ウ
も ン

Clouds　云 ⇨  ＋ 雫　Rain

the original character
原字　Genji

	Shell-and-bone Script 甲骨文 Kokotsubun	甲骨文字 Kokotsumoji 14c - 11c B.C.
雲	Seal 篆 Ten	篆書 Tensho 11c - 3c B.C.
雲	Clerical 隷 Rei	隷書 Reisho 3 B.C. - 3 A.D.

◁ - - - - - - - - - - - - - (楷 Kai？) See p56

雲	Running, Semi-cursive 行 Gyo	行書 Gyosho 1c - 3c A.D.
雲	Cursive, Grass, Rough 草 So	草書 Sosho Began 2c A.D.
雲	Standard, Formal, Regular 楷 Kai	楷書 Kaisho Began 3c A.D.

The eight strokes of the character "Ei (Yung 永)"
Eiji happo (Yung-Tzu-Pa-Fa 永字八法)
Wang Hsi-chih (王羲之) 4c.

1) Soku （Tse 側） to slant
2) Roku （Le 勒）   to bridle
3) Do   （Nu 努）   to strive
4) Teki （Yo 趯）   to spring
5) Saku （Ts'e 策） to whip
6) Ryaku （Liao 掠） to skim
7) Taku （Cho 啄）   to peck
8) Taku （Chieh 磔） to tear

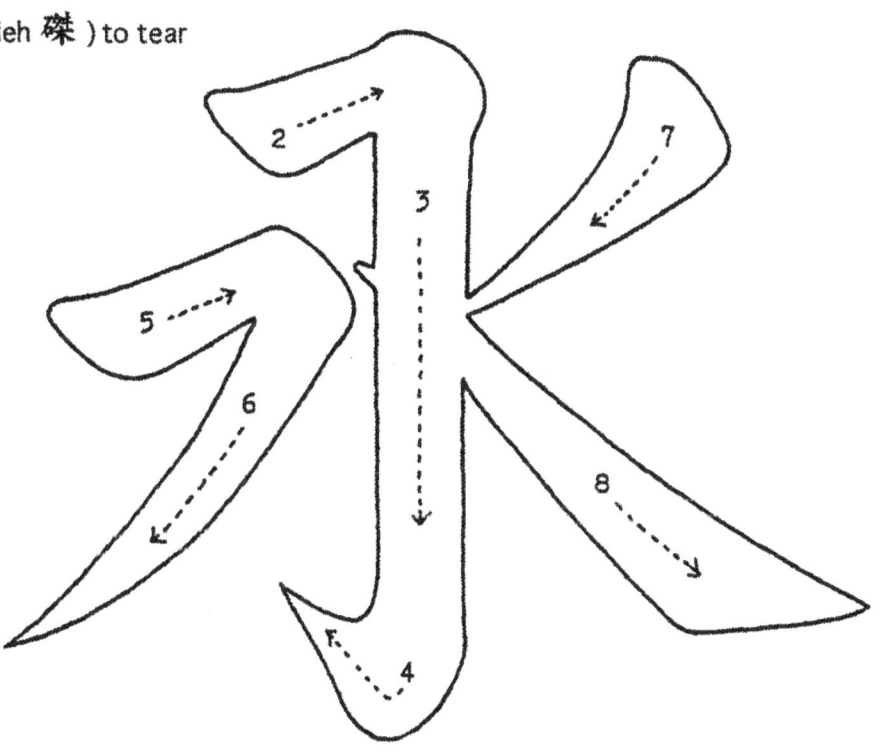

bird

鳥

cho
tori

is the hieroglyphic character representing " a bird".

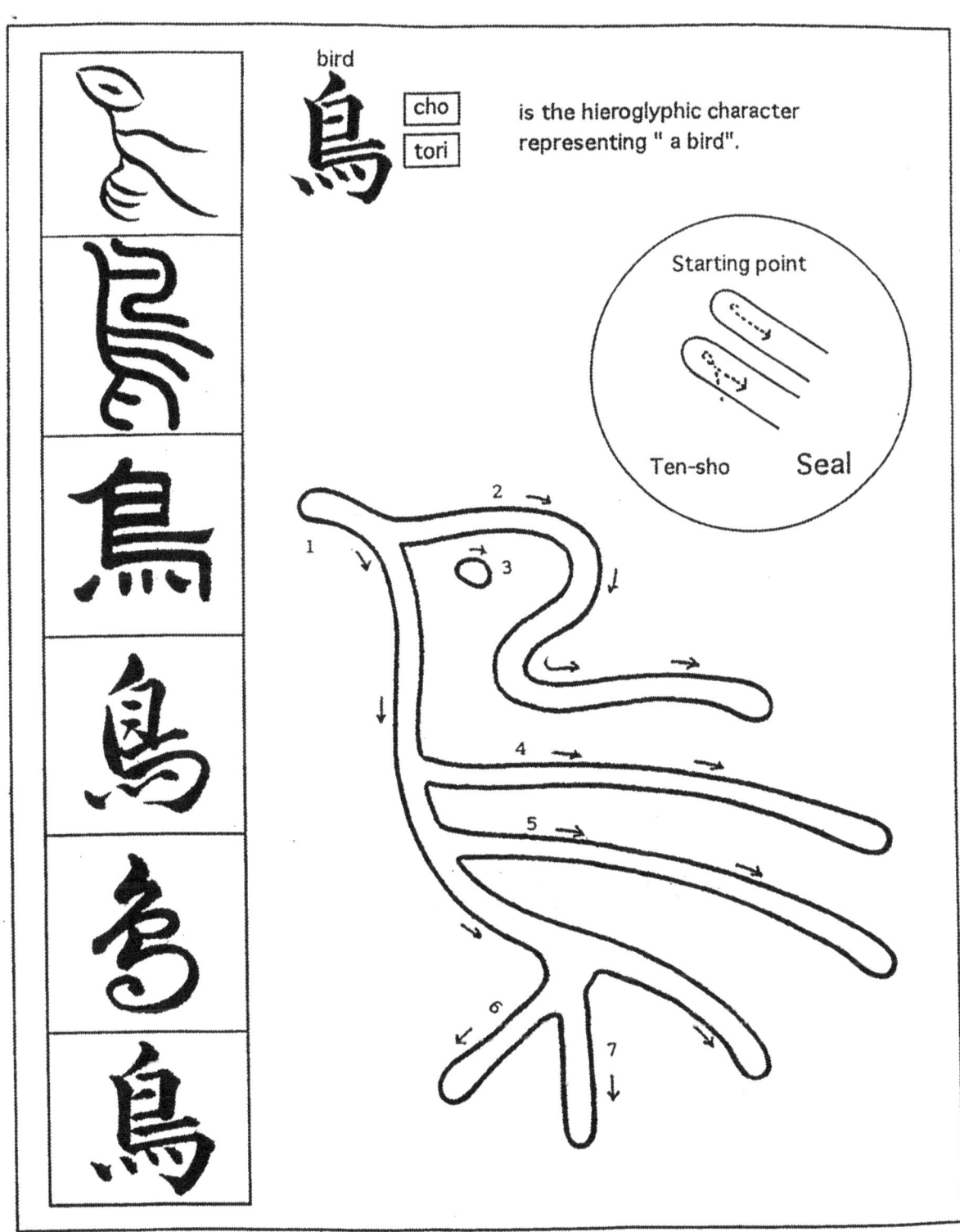

Starting point

Ten-sho   Seal

* Ei fujin, Madam Wei (衛夫人), 3rd - 4th Century
A T'ang Dynasty calligrapher describes her calligraphic style thus: "Like a fairy playing with shadows, a red lotus flower reflected on the pond." (Ch'en) A well known couplet reads "I first studied the calligraphy of Madam Wei, but alas I never succeeded in surpassing Wang Hsi Chih!"

For we look at strokes and characters from an animistic point of view. Thus Lady Wei said:
In the writing of those who are skilful in giving strength to their strokes, the characters are 'bony'; in writing of those who are not thus skillful, the characters are 'fleshy' . Writing that has a great deal of bone and very little meat is called 'sinewy'; and writing that is full of flesh and has weak bones is called 'piggy'. Powerful and sinewy writing is divine; writing that has neither power nor sinews is like an invalid.

* Ou Gi Shi, Wang Hsi Chih (王羲之), 307 - 365 (303 - 379)
A general in the court of Tsin (晋) Dynasty generally considered the greatest calligrapher of all time. He was particularly remembered for the Lan T'ing Hsu (蘭亭序), (Orchid Pavilion Preface), the authenticity of which is currently the subject of heated dispute. His calligraphy was described as being "Like a dragon scaling Heaven's gate and a tiger lying at rest in a phoenix's chamber." He was extremely fond of swans and was often persuaded to write in return for gift of a swan. In fact, some say that his calligraphic style was inspired by the graceful movements of that bird.

Three of the Greatest Calligraphers in the Early Tang Dynasty
(初唐の三大書家)

1) Ou Yo Jun, Ou-Yang Hsun (歐陽詢)

2) Gu Sei Nan, Yu Shih-Nan (虞世南)

3) Cho Sui Ryo, Ch'u Sui-Liang (褚遂良)

1)

2)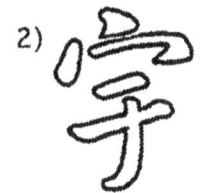

Four of the Greatest Calligraphers of the Tang Dynasty
（唐の四大書家）

1) Ou Yo Jun, Ou-Yang Hsun (歐陽詢) 557-641

2) Gu Sei Nan, Yu Shih-Nan (虞世南) 558-638

3) Cho Sui Ryo, Ch'u Sui-Liang (褚遂良) 596-658

4) Gan Shin Kei, Yen-Chen-Ch'ing (顏真卿) 709-785

NOTE:

Tang（唐）618-907

3)

4)
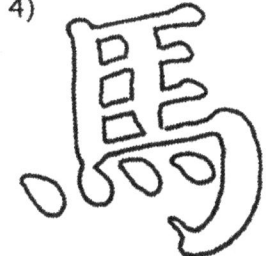

73

The Three Section of the Horizontal Stroke called "ichi (yokoichi)" are:

1) KI-HITSU   （起筆） the Starting Stroke

    SHI-HITSU   （始筆）

2) SO-HITSU   （送筆） the Sending Stroke

3) SHU-HITSU   （収筆） the Ending Stroke

             （終筆）

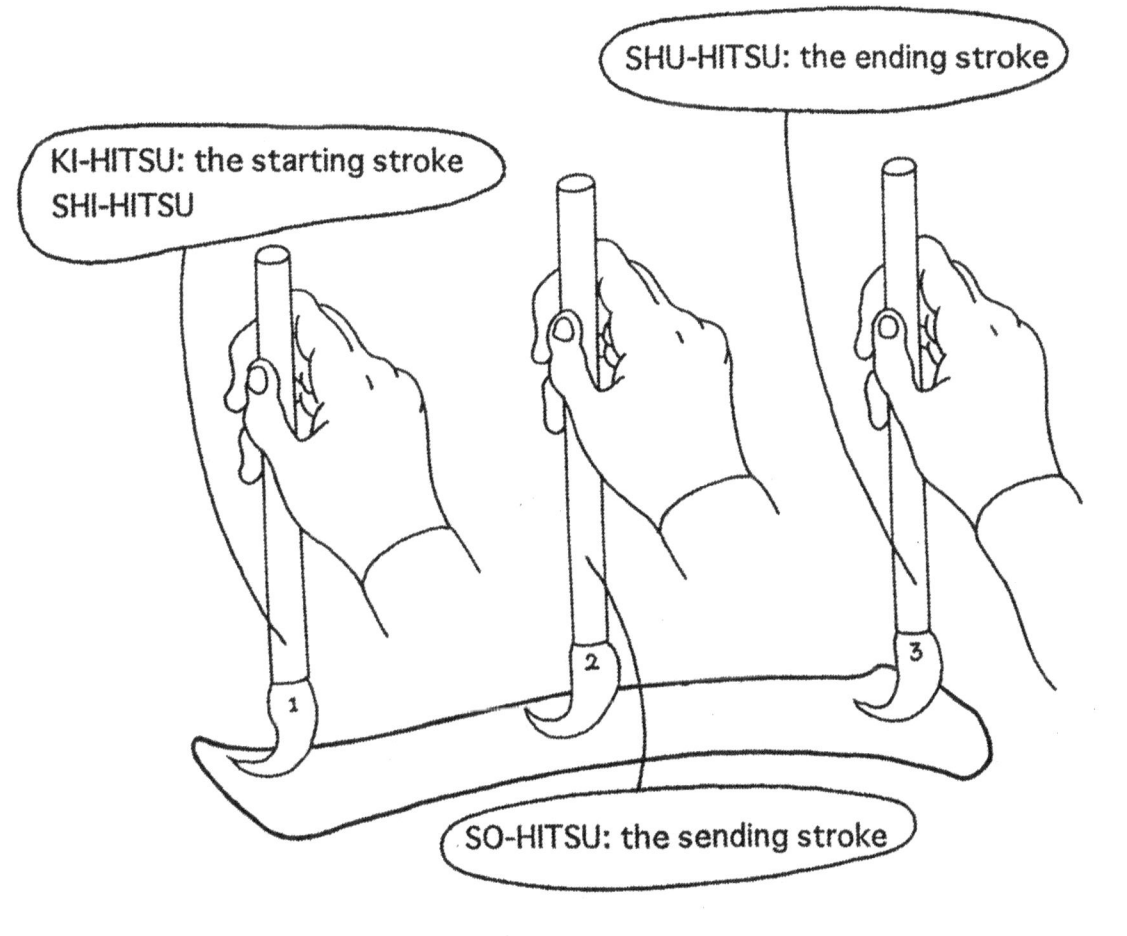

How to create perfect ink on an inkstone!

Take a good quality inkstick and rub it tenderly on the wetted surface of the inkstone in tender round circles. Be cautious not to scratch the inkstone. In Japan we often say "It is best for a lady instead of a fellow to grind an inkstick on the inkstone to make ink, because ladies have a tender hand". If we are careless and grind too firmly, we will have rough granulated ink instead of fine granulated ink. An inkstick is made of soot and cow-skin glue. Please handle an inkstick and an inkstone like your baby son or baby daughter, tender even pressure.

There are two ways of holding an inkstick!

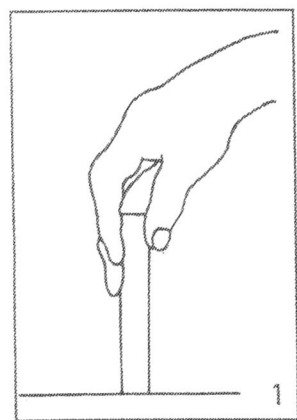

1) the Vertical Manner (Chokkaku-ho 直角法)

In general, this is the holding manner for a small inkstick. At first, make circles a few times on the surface of a wetted inkstone, and rub the whole area of the hill of the inkstone. Then the dark ink on the hill of the inkstone will gradually be pushed down into the ink pond. Dip fresh water out of the pond with the inkstone on to the hill, after rubbing the sur face of the inkstone again several more times, the whole procedure repeats.

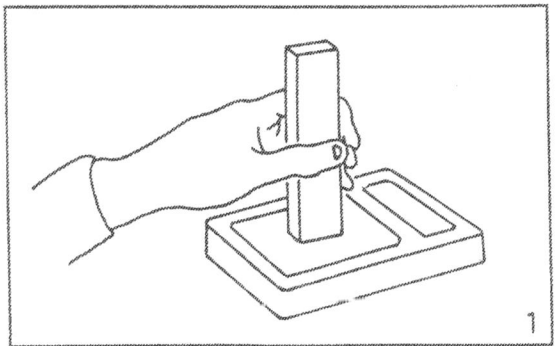

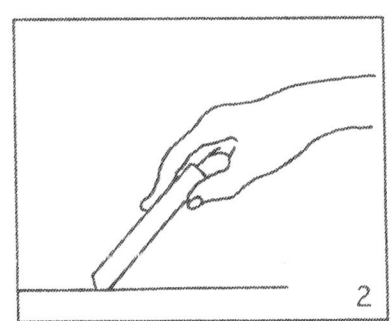

2) the Slanting Manner (Shakaku-ho 斜角法)

This holding manner will be applied by using a long inkstick. This way is easier for us to grind an inkstick on the surface of an inkstone. We will achieve finer granules by the slanting angle holding of a large inkstick.

Dimensions and Shapes of Calligraphy Rice Papers

1) Tanzaku （短冊）: Ode-paper, Exclamation on memo size paper 10" x 3.5" or bigger.

2) Shikishi （色紙）: poem-paper about 10" x 10" or bigger.

3) Hanshi （半紙）: Common Japanese writing paper for practicing 13" x 9.5".

4) Jofuku （条副）: Vertical-cut-paper about 57" x 16.5".

   Hansetsu （半折）: Cut in two about 57" x 16.5".

5) Zenshi （全紙）: Large paper about 57" x 33" or bigger.

6) Senmen （扇面）: Fan shaped rice paper about 7.5" x 20".

* Above different shaped rice papers are applied for calligraphy and painting.

1) Tanzaku: Ode-paper, rectangular rice paper applying for Waka (Japanese poem) and Haiku (Japanese poem has a seasonal ward, syllabled 5-7-5).

2) Shikishi: Poem-paper is used for painting and poem writing.

3) Hanshi: Common Japanese writing paper for practicing to write Chinese charac ters and Hiragana and Katakana. This is only used for practicing purpose, not for art exhibition purposes.

4) Jofuku or Hansetsu: Vertical-cut-paper

This is applied for Chinese characters and Kana (Japanese syllabary) and, Chinese and Japanese brush painting.

5) Zenshi: Large size paper, Zenshi is used for all purposes.

6) Senmen: Fan shaped rice paper

This is applied for Chinese characters and poem-writing and brush paint ing with ink or water color.

1) Tanzaku   2) Shikishi   3) Hanshi   4) Jofuku Hansetsu   5) Zenshi

6) Senmen

Three Different Angles of Holding a Bamboo Brush When Writing a Character

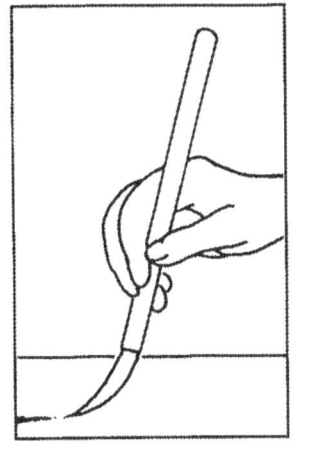

ex. 1

(1) JUN-HITSU (順筆 the Slant Brush)
This technique facilitates to express the naturalness, calmness and smoothness very much.

My drawing is an example of a vertical stroke, it shows the above mentioned quality.

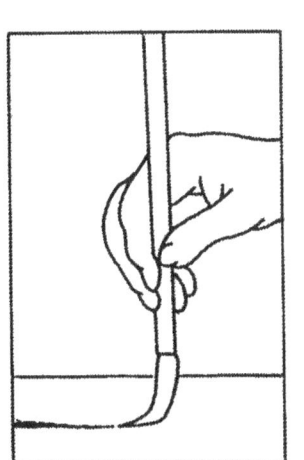

ex. 2

(2) CHOKU-HITSU (直筆 the Vertical Brush)
This is a stronger stroke than (1) JUN-HITSU. With it, it is easier to express lighter feeling, straighter and stronger stroke. This assures a quality line with a clean edge.

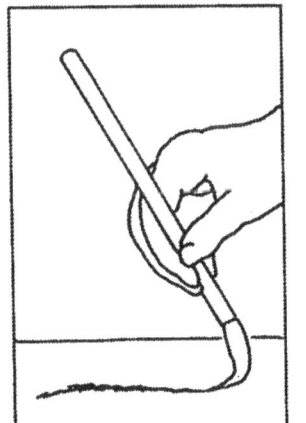

ex. 3

(3) GYAKU-HITSU (逆筆 the Reverse Angle of the Brush)
This is a much stronger stroke than (1) and (2). This easily expresses a rough quality line, it achieves a split brush or a dry brush effect. And also in this manner, you can achieve a narrower as well as a thicker stroke, drifting into a wider or narrower stroke.

Three Slightly Different Kinds of the Vertical Strokes of the Same Character

ex. hi (the sun, sunlight, a day, a date)

1) CHOKU-SEI (直勢) has the vertical parallel strokes with straight lines.

ex. (1)

2) HAI-SEI (背勢) expresses our term of CONCAVE.

ex. (2)

3) KO-SEI (向勢) indicates the term of CONVEX.

ex. (3)

Comparison between Three Kanji Calligraphic Styles and Hiragana (Japanese syllabary)

1) **Kai-sho (楷書): Standard style**
   Probably Kaisho began to be used around at the end of the Late Han Dynasty (25-220 A.D.).
   Kai-sho has different names. These names are Shin-sho (真書), Sei-sho (正書), Shin-ji (真字) & Mana (真名). The word of "Kai 楷" is the name of an evergreen tree that has straight branches. People say that Kaisho's form is like a standing man. In Kaisho style, we write strokes of the characters precisely. Once you put your brush down to the rice paper, you must complete the character without correction.

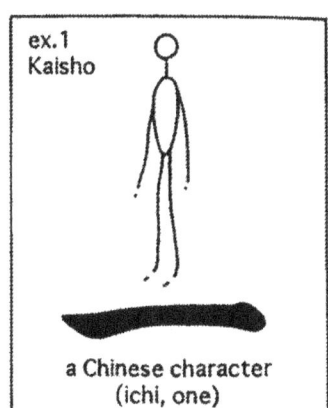

ex.1
Kaisho

a Chinese character
(ichi, one)

2) **Gyo-sho (行書): Semi-cursive style**
   Gyosho means "This script is used by general public widely", and was invented by Ryu Toku Sho (Liu Tesheng 劉德昇), so said a legend. Gyosho is formed by abbreviation of Kaisho strokes.

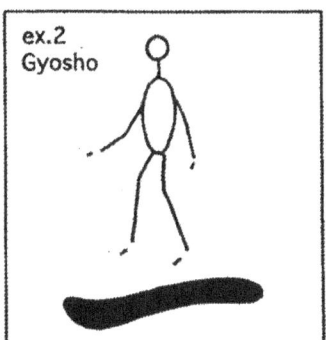

ex.2
Gyosho

3) **So-sho (草書): Cursive style, Grass**
   Sosho has a meaning of "Grass or quick writing, shorthand. Sosho has a different name, called "Konso (今草)", was made by Cho Shi (張芝 Chang Chih) in the Late Han Dynasty (25-220 A.D.) as by a legend. Sosho formed by the abbreviation of the clerical. The origin of Sosho (Cursive style) was derived from the beginning of the Han Dynasty (206 B.C. - 220 A.D.)

ex.3
Sosho

4) **Hiragana (平仮名 Japanese syllabary)**
   Hiragana was created by the Cursive style of the Chinese characters.

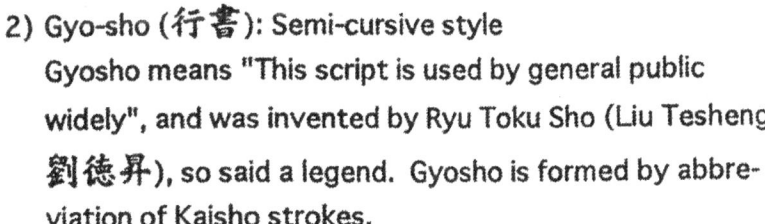

⇨

(Hiragana, tsu)

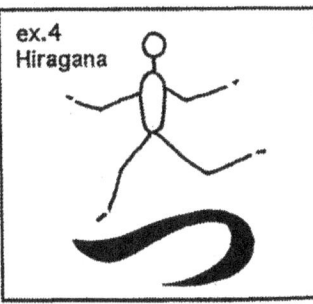

ex.4
Hiragana

The different brush strokes by three old masters during the Tang Dynasty (618-906)

ex. (1) O-HO	ex. (2) CHO-HO	ex. (3) GAN-PO

 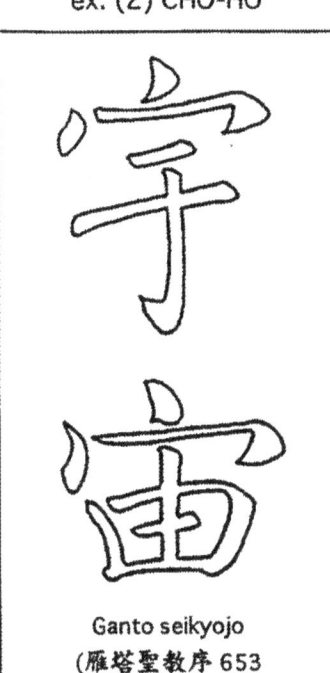 

Kyuseikyu rei sen no mei	Ganto seikyojo	Hoseichijo
(九成宮醴泉銘 632	(雁塔聖教序 653	(放生池帖 8c
Jiuchenggong Liquan Ming)	Yanta Sheng Chiao Hsu)	Fang Sheng Chi Tieh)

* The above three "Uchu" examples mean "the universe, the cosmos".

1) O-HO (歐法 O-manner): (Ou-Yang Hsun (歐陽詢) 557-641)

Probably, O Yo Jun (歐陽詢) is number one calligrapher in Standard style through out ancient and modern times. Tang dynasty art critics said "O's writing is like a snake in the bush, it is a surprise like a flash of lightning in the clouds. His writing is very impressive.

2) CHO-HO (褚法 Cho-manner): (Ch'u Sui-Liang (褚遂良) 596-658)

One of Tang critics sees in Cho's calligraphy as lively written golden characters which shine as rows of colorful precious gems.

3) GAN-PO (顏法 Gan-manner): (Yen-Chen-Ch'ing (顏真卿) 709-785)

In Japan, Japanese calligraphers often say "Gan's manner of writing is very powerful, energetic and strong. The structure of his characters resembles the Japanese Sumo wrestlers.

Three Kinds of Basic Horizontal and Vertical Strokes during the T'ang Dynasty (618-906)

> 1) O-HO (歐法 O-manner): (Ou-Yang Hsun (歐陽詢)'s manner 557-641)
>
> 2) CHO-HO (褚法 Cho-manner): (Ch'u Sui-Liang (褚遂良)'s manner 596-658)
>
> 3) GAN-PO (顏法 Gan-manner): (Yen-Chen-Ch'ing (顏真卿)'s manner 709-785)

1) The O-HO (O-manner) is recognized by keeping the same pressure from the starting stroke on to the ending stroke.

ex. (1)

2) The CHO-HO   has heavy pressure at the starting stroke and again at the ending stroke. At the sending stroke, you draw the stroke much faster, resulting in a sharper stroke, but thinner.

ex. (2)

3) The GAN-PO   shows normal pressure at the starting stroke, and also at the ending stroke. But the sending stroke recieves much more pressure resulting in a stronger image.

ex. (3)

Gan Shin Kei (顏真卿 Yen-Chen-Ch'ing 709-785)

* The following examples are to indicate the variety of Gan's calligraphic style. Please find out the sifference between a,b,c....and g.

1) The Chinese character " 天 ten" has a meaning of "heaven".

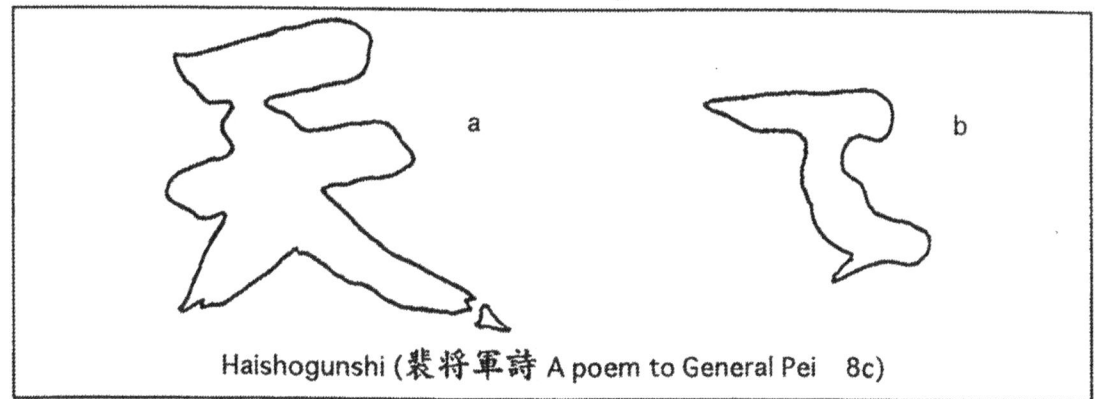

Haishogunshi (裴将軍詩 A poem to General Pei   8c)

Hoseichijo (放生池帖 Fang Shen Chi Tieh   8c)

2) The Chinese character " 六 roku" has a meaning of "six".

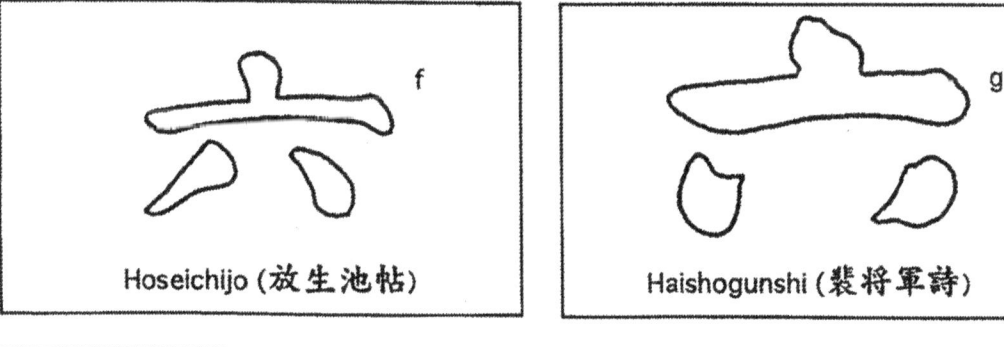

Hoseichijo (放生池帖)   Haishogunshi (裴将軍詩)

This is a good example of the normal standard style writing of the Kanji "yama 山".

san, yama
mountain

ex. 山

These are three bad examples of standard writing of the character 'yama 山'.

1) Sa-ji 左字 (the left-handed character)

Kyoji 鏡字 (the mirror character)

Kyoei-moji 鏡映文字
(the character reflecting in the mirror)

* This looks as if written by a lefthanded person, a reversed calligraphy character.

ex.

2) Taore-ji 倒れ字 (the falling down character)

Keisha-moji 傾斜文字 (the slanting character)

* This is a slanting character. We consider that this is one of the bad examples of the unusual characters.

ex.

3) Utsubo-ji うつぼ字(靫字)
(the arrow case character)

* This means a written character like an arrow case which has an empty space inside the case. Thus, the written character does not have depth.

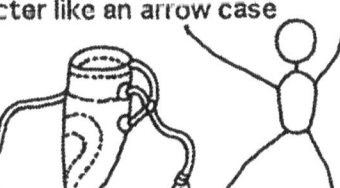

ex.

As a calligraphy beginner student (1)

You should not have a preference for unusual images.

When a beginner has a chance to see the skilled calligraphers writings of techniques by Sa-ji, Taore-ji and Utsubo-ji , the beginner is often jealous of the calligrapher's work, because his written characters have a kind of special expression. However it is easy for the beginner to copy this type of characters if he knows certain secrets how to write expressive characters. The total populace discusses this subject intensely, thus, a beginner oneself recognizes that the main stream, makes light of the basic fundamental practice to write characters. Please try not to imitate this unfortunate trend.

The calligraphic writing by the person who likes an unusual image occasionally but rarely is good. But in order to practice writing characters seriously, his writing tends to become now and then poor quality. Of course that is not his intention.

The main stream of practicing characters is to practice characters beautifully, exactly and repeatedly. The right way of calligraphy is a long and difficult task to accomplish. Especially, a talented person often to drift into the wrong course. Please try to keep on the right course.

1) Sa-ji 左字 (the left-handed character) Kyoji 鏡字 (the mirror character)

2) Taore-ji 倒れ字 (the falling down character) Keisha-moji 傾斜文字 (the slanting character)

3) Utsubo-ji うつぼ字 (靫字) (the arrow case character)

ex.
1) Sa-ji　　　　　　　2) Taore-ji　　　　　　　3) Utsubo-ji

As a calligraphy beginner student (2)

You often experience good and bad mood while practicing to write characters, while being a calligraphy beginner student.

When you practice to write characters, you often feel that your characters do not live up to the good quality you have in mind to achieve. Then your written characters are not similar to the sample calligraphy. At this still incomplete character writing ability, you can not write characters the way you want to. Then you will develop a trend to dislike to practice writing characters and you will get into the habit of ignoring practicing. However, you can guard against such a state of personal attitude by continuing to practice without changing the basic calligraphic manner. Your negative attitude will disappear in a matter of a few days, according to "the Junbokusho (入木抄)", in four to ten days. After this difficult period, you will be able to write much better characters than you did before. After passing through this period, you will enjoy writing masterly drawn characters. And your studying calligraphy will be a most present pastime. Try to make this enjoyable pastime to continue from month to come.

The above is an extraction from the book of Jubokusho " 入木抄 "
by Prince Sonen (尊円親王 1298-1356)

* Good example of hoding a brush

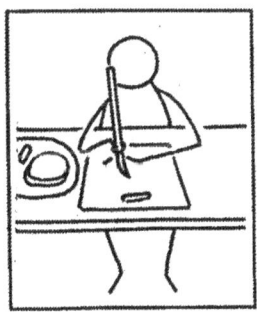 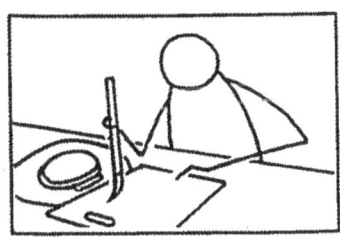 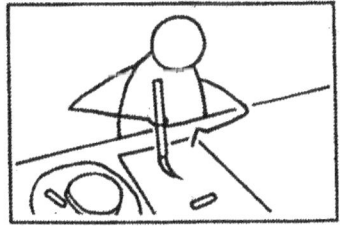

CHINESE DYNASTIES

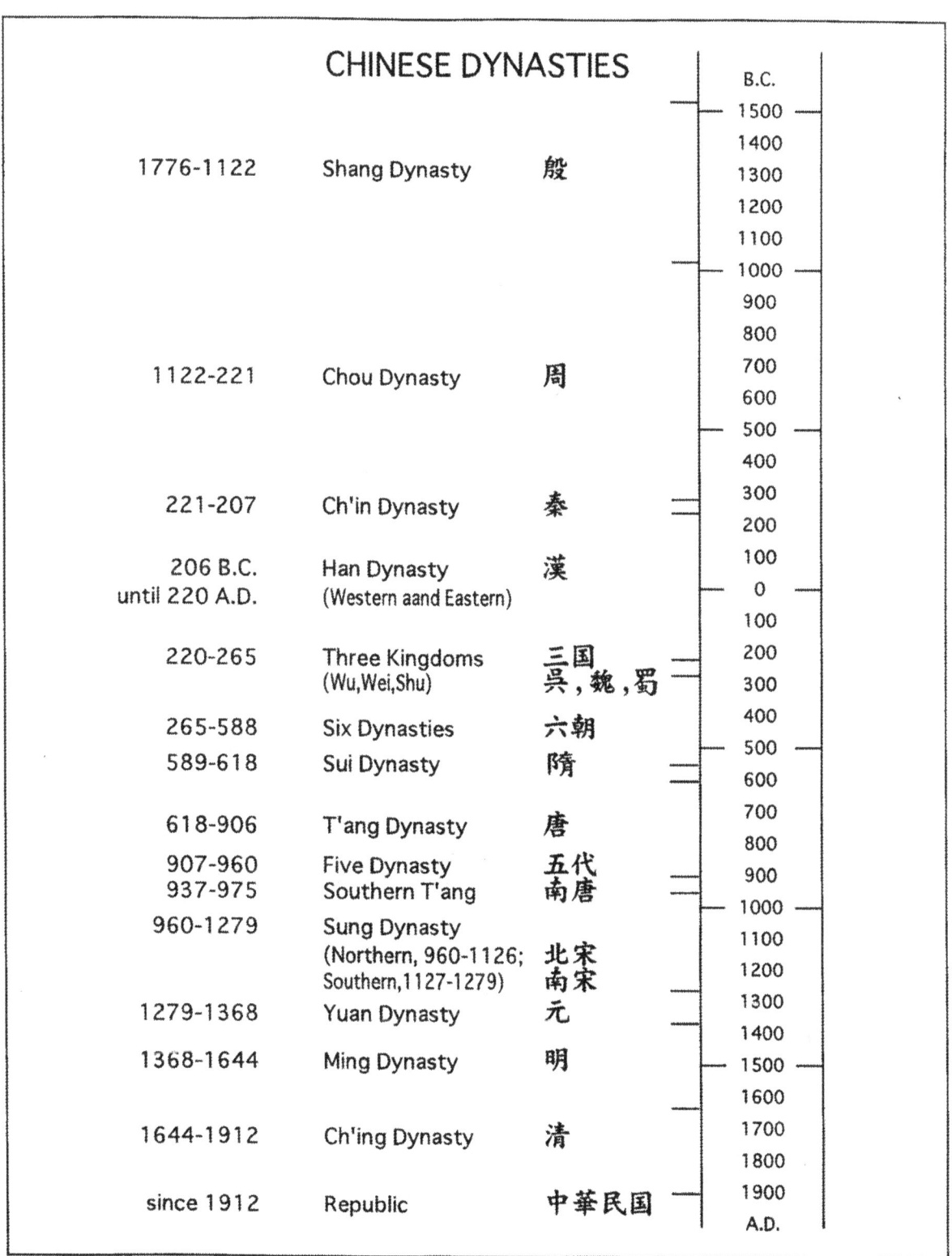

			B.C.
			1500
			1400
1776-1122	Shang Dynasty	殷	1300
			1200
			1100
			1000
			900
			800
1122-221	Chou Dynasty	周	700
			600
			500
			400
221-207	Ch'in Dynasty	秦	300
			200
206 B.C.	Han Dynasty	漢	100
until 220 A.D.	(Western aand Eastern)		0
			100
220-265	Three Kingdoms	三国	200
	(Wu,Wei,Shu)	吳,魏,蜀	300
265-588	Six Dynasties	六朝	400
589-618	Sui Dynasty	隋	500
			600
618-906	T'ang Dynasty	唐	700
			800
907-960	Five Dynasty	五代	900
937-975	Southern T'ang	南唐	1000
960-1279	Sung Dynasty		1100
	(Northern, 960-1126;	北宋	1200
	Southern,1127-1279)	南宋	1300
1279-1368	Yuan Dynasty	元	1400
1368-1644	Ming Dynasty	明	1500
			1600
1644-1912	Ch'ing Dynasty	清	1700
			1800
since 1912	Republic	中華民国	1900
			A.D.

About the Author

Hideo Muranaka received his BFA and MFA from the Tokyo National University of Fine Arts and Music in 1970, 1972.

His pencil drawing was selected and he was invited to participate with **The Pacific Coast States Collection from the Vice President's House** at the Vice President's House, Washington, D.C., 1980, and exhibited at the National Museum of American Art, 1981. His drawing (pencil, ink) was awarded the Second Prize from the International Art Exhibition for MUSEO HOSIO in 1984 and First Prize, 1988, Italy. His calligraphy was awarded the First Prize from the Nogijinja (general Nogi Shrine) Calligraphy Exhibition, called "Kensho" in 1961 and the numerous others.

Biographical data: *Who's Who is American Art*, 17th Edition, 1986; *Men of Achievement*, 1988, England, etc.

www.ingramcontent.com/pod-product-compliance
Lightning Source LLC
Chambersburg PA
CBHW081222280526
45787CB00006B/2492